VALUES-DRIVEN AUTHENTIC LEADERSHIP

VALUES-DRIVEN AUTHENTIC LEADERSHIP

Essential Lessons from the
LeadershipWWEB Podcast Series

Andrew Braham
Matthew Waller
John English

Foreword by John White

FAYETTEVILLE
2022

ISBN: 978-1-95489-206-4
eISBN: 978-1-95489-207-1

26 25 24 23 22 5 4 3 2 1

∞ The paper used in this publication meets the minimum requirements of the American National Standard for Permanence of Paper for Printed Library Materials Z39.48-1984.

Library of Congress Control Number: 2021951928

To John White, the first "W" in LeadershipWWEB.

CONTENTS

Filling a Vacuum in Leadership Literature

*V*alues-Driven Authentic Leadership fills a vacuum in leadership literature, and it does so by employing a student- or leader-driven process. Feedback from students after listening to podcast recordings with a diverse set of leaders established the framework for the book. Lessons learned from leaders who were interviewed and research performed on authentic leadership provided the book's content. What makes the book stand apart from others is its focus on values.

In many ways, the book is a by-product of a leadership course I created at the University of Arkansas. The course, Leadership Principles and Practices, was designed initially for graduate students, with a limited number of seniors permitted to enroll after being interviewed by me. Over time, as word spread, the number of seniors enrolled in the course increased significantly. When it was last offered, 63 percent of the students enrolled in the course were undergraduates.

The leadership class met on Tuesday evenings from 6:00 p.m. until 8:50 p.m., with a midsession break. Fifteen of the sixteen class meetings included a guest leader during the first half of the class period. The second half was devoted to discussions of assigned leadership books and my integrating my leadership journey with what guest leaders and leadership books said.

Guest leaders did not prepare presentations. Instead, they responded to questions posed by me and class participants. Drawn from academe, athletics, business, government, and nonprofit organizations, they held mid- to top-level leadership positions. Students were amazed at the level of candor from guest leaders as they responded to students' questions.

Without question, the major attraction of the course was that it gave students the opportunity to ask leaders anything they wanted. As the students prepared to be launched into their next phase of life, they were anxious to receive advice from people who had successfully negotiated the transition from school to work. The postmillennials were interested not only in how to become successful leaders, but also in how to achieve their life goals—which included how to become a values-driven authentic leader.

Based on feedback from students he recommended take the course, Andrew Braham asked if he could attend class meetings. I readily agreed. As Andrew observed and participated in class discussions, he identified a theme in the questions students asked: values-driven leadership. As the time approached for me to retire, Andrew approached me and the deans of the colleges of business and engineering—Matthew Waller and John English, respectively—with a proposal: create a series of podcast recordings focused on values. We did so, with many of the twenty-three recordings coming from interviews of leaders who had met with my leadership class.

Based on feedback from students who listened to the recordings, Andrew asked John, Matt, and me to work with him in writing a book on values-based leadership. Because I was already committed to writing a book on leadership and wanted to avoid any appearance of a conflict of interest, I declined. Fortunately, Andrew, John, and Matt stayed the course and have produced *Values-Driven Authentic Leadership*. In so doing, they identified six opportunities when reliance on one's core values is critical: having a mentor; being in a group; leading yourself; transitions; being a mentor; and values and company culture. The five opportunities serve as a framework for the eight-chapter book. Drawing on the work of Peter Northouse, Bill George, Steven Sample, and others, they combine values-based leadership with authentic leadership.

Mentorship and its importance were addressed numerous times by leaders who were interviewed. Thus, it is not surprising to find the subject of mentoring serving as bookends for the book, with the second chapter addressing having a mentor and the sixth chapter devoted to being a mentor. In between, the third chapter examines the challenges of and opportunities for being a leader and being a team member. The fourth chapter examines the need for living your core values, being yourself, and being an authentic leader. The fifth chapter addresses transitions, dealing with personal and professional change. The penultimate chapter addresses the opposite side of the mentoring coin, being a mentor. The seventh chapter returns to values-based leadership and addresses relationships between personal core values and an organization's core values, emphasizing the need for their alignment. The book closes with the authors sharing the inspiration they have received from leaders and summarizing their views on values-driven authentic leadership.

Prior to the interviews, each leader was asked to identify his or her top five values. There was no guidance provided on whether these were personal, professional, or leadership values, which generated a diverse list of answers. Collectively, the twenty-three leaders interviewed cited fifty-two values. Integrity was the most frequently cited core value. The other values included in the top five were authenticity, service, vision, and developing people. The authors weave the five values together in creating a tapestry titled *Values-Driven Authentic Leadership*.

The interviews reinforced the importance of having a leader's core values align with an organization's core values. Several leaders discussed their personal core values and how those were aligned with the core values of the organizations they led. When a mismatch existed, several leaders chose to leave and find an organization whose core values were aligned with theirs.

To be an authentic leader, the authors emphasize the need to be true to yourself and your core values; to be transparent and balanced; to have a compelling vision for the organization you lead; and to know your strengths and weaknesses, as well as those of the people you lead.

The model recommended by the authors for effective authentic leadership is servant leadership. A key component of servant leadership is investing in and developing the people you lead. Many leaders interviewed provided examples of servant leadership in practice.

Bringing the book to a close, the authors state, "So what have we learned? Leaders inspire us." They cite several things that leaders inspired them to do. As you read *Values-Driven Authentic Leadership*, you will be inspired to be more values-driven in your leadership and to be a more authentic leader. Why am I confident that this will happen? It happened to me. Happy reading!

John White, chancellor emeritus,
University of Arkansas, May 2021

ACKNOWLEDGMENTS

Thank you to John White, Chris McCoy, Shelley Simpson, Mike Duke, Donnie Smith, Kim LaScola Needy, John Reap, Troy Alley, John N. Roberts III, Mike Johnson, Pam McGinnis, Jessica Hendrix, Angela J. Grayson, Anthony J. Vinciquerra, J. R. Jones, Greg Brown, Charles Robinson, Scott Bennett, Sam Alley, Mario Ramirez, Kelly Barnes, and Stu Todd. You provided the vast majority of the material for this book. We walked away from every LeadershipWWEB podcast recording thinking "wow," "humbling," "impressive," and "staggering." You inspire us to continue our leadership journey.

Thank you also to Bryan Hill, Rachel Pohl, and Sadie Casillas for helping us with the podcast recordings. You added a unique and valuable perspective to our discussions with each guest, and we appreciate your contributions.

Finally, a huge thank you to Loray Mosher for her assistance with the postproduction of the podcasts and Stephen Caldwell for his assistance with editing the book. You took our content to the next level and made it great!

The Birth of LeadershipWWEB

Andrew Braham

There was no reason to suspect that the fall of 2013 would have a transformative impact on my leadership journey, much less that the events of that year would lead to the book you are holding.

The seeds of my approach to leadership had been planted about a decade earlier, when I worked with Koch Materials Company (KMC). At the time, KMC was a stand-alone pavement materials company and owned by Koch Industries, which is based in Wichita, Kansas. KMC offered all of its employees internal training that was based on the theory of market-based management (Koch 2007). Everyone was given a Koch principles bookmark in the packet of training program resources, and this bookmark is still posted on a wall in my office.[1]

The shoots of my leadership emerged from the soil in 2007–8, while I was working at the Illinois Leadership Center as a graduate student at the University of Illinois at Urbana-Champaign.[2] The center's cornerstone initiative is its leadership training known as the I-Programs, which I took part in with great enthusiasm. There are seven I-Programs now, but in my day there were four.[3] Each was a six-hour seminar that focused on a particular aspect of leadership practice.

---

1. The ten principles from 2003 on the bookmark are: act with integrity, apply market-based management, develop decision-making capabilities, set high expectations, build relationships, practice humility and honesty, treat others with dignity and respect, freely share your knowledge, challenge the status quo, and have work become a major focus of life.
2. For the center's website, see https://illinois.edu/about/index.html.
3. Integrity, intersect, imprint, and ignite.

My leadership growth, however, was turbocharged in fall 2013 with two events.

The first happened, of all places, in a spin class (a bicycle workout) at a gym in Fayetteville, Arkansas.

Students in a spin class aren't assigned a bike, but the regulars gravitate to the same seats for each session. Naturally, you get to know the people around you. I began chatting with the gentleman next to me one morning and found that, like me, he worked at the University of Arkansas. I was an assistant professor at the time (I was just beginning my academic career), while my new friend, Matt Waller, was the chair (the first level of administration at a university) of the Supply Chain Management Department.

Over the course of a couple of weeks of chatting before and after the spin class, I found it very easy to talk with Matt and that he always had good insights on whatever topic we were covering. So one day I asked if he would consider becoming my mentor. The first sign that ours would be a strong relationship was that he asked to think about it. I now realize that he was thinking of a long-term commitment, not just a meeting here and there. The next time we met, Matt said he would be my mentor, and nine years later, this book became one of the fruits of our relationship.

The second pivotal event that fall involved John White, the former chancellor of the University of Arkansas and a distinguished professor of industrial engineering. John was teaching his Leadership Principles and Practices course, and I had heard from both students and faculty that it was phenomenal. I asked John if my wife and I could sit in on the class, and he enthusiastically agreed to let us attend. He even made name cards for us, just like every graduate student. Over the course of the sixteen-week semester, we were treated to John's vast knowledge of leadership, read eight books, and listened to his conversations with fifteen invited speakers—CEOs, corporate presidents, chancellors, athletic directors, generals, and other leaders.

My experiences in John's leadership course, along with what I had learned at KMC and the Illinois Leadership Center, provided much of the foundation for my mentoring relationship with Matt. In each of our monthly meetings, we spent half the time just chatting and the other half discussing a leadership book, article, or blog. As we all know, there is an endless source of information on leadership available, and Matt and I devoured what we could over the years.

From Bikes to a Podcast Series to a Book

Matt moved from department chair to associate dean for executive education and then dean of the Sam M. Walton College of Business. During each transition, I offered to put aside our mentor-mentee relationship, but each time he said that he was getting as much, if not more, out of it than I was.

During the summer of 2018, Matt mentioned that one of his goals as dean was to write a book a year—and that he would like me to be a coauthor of one of those books. I was honored to have such an opportunity, and I jumped at the chance.

Since we had spent so much of the previous five years discussing leadership, a book on that topic seemed very appropriate. There already are thousands of leadership books, however, so we wondered what new perspective we could bring to the table. One thing we agreed on was the importance of values in leadership. Often, when all other leadership tools fail, your core values are the one thing that remains to shape your actions. Interestingly, while many of the books, articles, and blogs that we read had flavors of values, almost none of them focused exclusively on values.

With this in mind, we moved forward with the idea of a leadership book based on values. And the more we talked about it, the more we found ourselves discussing all the different people with strong, clearly defined values who had influenced our leadership journeys.

What if we interviewed some of those leaders to get their perspectives on values-based leadership? we thought. But why stop there? If we were going to interview them, why not record the discussions, turn them into a podcast, and share what we learned with others?

At this point, we were really excited. But we also realized we would miss a lot of opportunities if we limited the project to the two of us, so we reached out to John White and John English, who at the time was dean of the University of Arkansas's College of Engineering.

On Tuesday, August 29, 2018, the four of us met in John English's office. Matt and I proposed a joint project by the engineering and business colleges that would produce a podcast series and book on values targeted to undergraduate students. We would dub the podcast "LeadershipWWEB," with "WWEB" representing our last names—White, Waller, English, and

Braham.[4] This was the first of many meetings that led to twenty-three podcasts and formed the foundation of this book.

Values, Opportunities, and a Framework of Leadership

The twenty-three LeadershipWWEB podcasts were recorded from October 2018 through December 2019, and we received a wealth of information. It quickly became apparent that we needed more than just a values-based leadership perspective, so we identified different opportunities in life when holding onto and applying your values are critical to developing and displaying strong leadership. The first five opportunities we found were:

- Having a mentor
- Being in a group
- Knowing yourself
- Navigating transitions
- Being a mentor

In addition, we were exposed to a wealth of information on the intersection of values and company culture. Therefore, we added "values and company culture" as an opportunity to explore how we could match organizational values with values provided during the podcasts—whether they are personal, leadership, or professional values.

You'll note that each opportunity is a chapter in this book. The first chapter, however, covers what we think of as global leadership. All four of us are academics, so we feel most comfortable working with an established, theoretical framework. We scoured the existing literature and decided that values-based leadership was most similar to authentic leadership, an accepted academic area of research that has been deemed independent enough from other areas of leadership to warrant its own arena.

I've come to see those three core constructs—values, opportunities, and the authentic leadership framework—as a tree. The trunk is authentic leadership (the solid foundation of the tree), each opportunity is a branch,

---

4. You can find the podcast by searching LeadershipWWEB on SoundCloud. A full list of the episodes—including the names of the guests, their positions at the time of the recording, and their top-five values, as well as the names of the interviewers—can be found in the appendix of this book.

Opportunity	Chapter
Having a mentor	2: Of Myths and Mentoring
Being in a group	3: Being a Team Player
Knowing yourself	4: Me, Myself, and I
Navigating transitions	5: Navigating Uncharted Waters
Being a mentor	6: The Importance of Mentoring
Values and company culture	7: Matching Company Values with Personal Values

Table I.1. Linking Opportunities to Chapters

and the values form the leaves on each branch. (This analogy may have its roots in Donnie Smith's metaphor of a peach tree, which you'll learn about in chapter 7.)

The values that our podcast guests discussed apply to all the different opportunities of leadership. Whether you have a mentor, are a mentor, or are sitting alone and reflecting on who you are, values apply to all facets of your work. Everything is held solidly together, however, by the concept of authentic leadership. These opportunities are linked to specific chapters as shown in Table I.1.

Chapter 1 describes the trunk of authentic leadership, and each opportunity is the focus of a subsequent chapter. Within each chapter there are "points to ponder" as you begin, a summary of how authentic leadership directly relates to the specific opportunity discussed in that chapter and how values are associated with it, and key takeaways from what you've read.

We have sprinkled in some of our own thoughts, and we'll share some personal stories along the way (breaking away from third person so you'll know which coauthor is sharing). But while White, Waller, English, and Braham (WWEB) began this endeavor, our guests provided the majority of the content. To say the least, we could not have written this book without them. The book, however, covers only a fraction of what our guests discussed. So while we hope you enjoy what you read in these pages, we also encourage you to listen to the podcasts. They provide a diverse and comprehensive analysis of values-based leadership.

We are thankful not only to our guests for their time and insights, but also to you for showing interest in this book. We hope you enjoy reading it as much as we enjoyed developing it. Perhaps it will become an unexpected marker in your leadership journey and something that will guide you for years to come.

Mining for Gold

Points to Ponder

- What are the four main categories of leadership?
- What are the six developing areas of leadership?
- What are the three perspectives of authentic leadership?
- How is authentic leadership related to values-based leadership concepts?

The LeadershipWWEB podcast was created as a forum for interviewing professionals from a variety of fields about their top five values and how those values shape their daily decisions. The objective of the podcast series and this book is to bring you a wide range of perspectives on leadership so you can either begin building your own leadership framework or enhance an existing framework.

After we recorded and published twenty-three episodes of the podcast, it became abundantly clear that the common themes expressed by the leaders were full of gold. We decided to mine the interviews and share the themes in a book about values-based leadership. And as we listened, read, researched, and wrote, we also began to explore how these values fit within the greater context of leadership theory.

As it turned out, they fit rather nicely, especially as it relates to authentic leadership. And this, we think, adds practical value for leaders while also contributing to the academic study of leadership.

Lifelong Leadership Learning

Leadership, of course, is not something you can become an expert on by reading one book. It is not a single goal you work toward and fully achieve. And it is not an idea that is static. Leadership is dynamic, changing, challenging, and exciting, and therefore it's always worth exploring in new ways.

Chris McCoy, a self-described student of leadership, exemplified this type of passion when he interviewed for the job of chief information officer (CIO) at the University of Arkansas. Chris was the only candidate who described in detail how he would manage and lead the university's information technology group from a framework of leadership and using leadership concepts. This was very impressive during the interview, but it was even more fun to watch after he was hired and implemented his ideas.

Chris did such a good job as CIO that he became the university's chief financial officer (CFO). Even though he had a relatively limited background in finance, he thrived as the CFO in part by implementing many of his leadership concepts.

One of the theories we will explore in this book is that when you get to certain positions in organizations, leadership skills are just as important as—if not more important than—technical skills. Highly competent technical expertise always exists within organizations, but strong leaders are needed to steer the ship in the right direction. The chancellor of the University of Arkansas was well aware of this when he interviewed Chris, and it made the decision to hire Chris as the CFO much easier.

Chris, who now is CIO for the University of North Texas System, keeps an office full of books on leadership because he is constantly trying to learn. During his podcast appearance, he named at least a dozen leadership books off the top of his head that he had read and studied to improve himself.

His leadership journey had its roots in the 1980s. Chris was working at Iowa State University, which hired Jim Nelson during that time to serve as dean of the college of engineering. Nelson had been a vice president of strategic planning of a company, and he had strong opinions when it came to strategic thought. *The Goal* by Eli Goldratt was one of Nelson's favorite books, and he recommended it to Chris. The book's discussions of the theory of constraints got Chris interested in leadership, so he moved on to *The Critical Chain* and *It's Not Luck*, both also by Goldratt, which deepened his understanding of strategic thought.

Chris also talked extensively about *The 21 Irrefutable Laws of Leadership*, by John Maxwell. After reading Maxwell, Chris was hooked. From then on, he led all his teams using a purposeful lens of leadership development.

A Global Understanding of Leadership

We share Chris's passion for lifelong learning, especially when it comes to leadership. So while this book is primarily focused on values, it is important to have a global understanding of leadership. A good place to start is with *Leadership: Theory and Practice*, an extremely comprehensive textbook by Peter Northouse (2018). Northouse defines four main categories of leadership:

1. Do as a leader wishes
2. Influence
3. Traits
4. Transformation

The first category, do as a leader wishes, has to do with getting followers to do what the leader wants. There is one person in charge who makes decisions, while everyone else follows. This category of leadership has many similarities to management.

The second category, influence, begins to distinguish leadership from management. Instead of a single person issuing orders and ultimatums, the person uses noncoercive methods to move the team in a particular direction. This allows team members to use their unique strengths while moving toward their goals.

The third category, traits, is based on *In Search of Excellence* by Tom Peters and Robert Waterman (2006). The authors identify five traits of a leader that are important for a team to thrive: intelligence, self-confidence, determination, integrity, and sociability.

Interestingly, the most common value provided during our LeadershipWWEB podcast discussions was integrity, with ten of the twenty-three guests identifying integrity as one of their top five values. Even more podcast discussions revolved around words found in the definition of integrity: honesty, trustworthiness, principles, and taking responsibility for actions.

The fourth category of leadership according to Northouse is "transformation," which occurs when a group of people engage with each other in a way that allows both leaders and followers to rise to higher levels of motivation and morality.

These four categories tend to define how a leader influences a group, but Northouse also discusses processes that are foundational to leadership.

Specifically, Northouse identified six developing areas of leadership that are increasingly being studied by academics. These developing areas are based more on the process of leadership rather than how a leader influences:

1. Authentic leadership
2. Spiritual leadership
3. Servant leadership
4. Adaptive leadership
5. Followership leadership
6. Discursive leadership

In the first developing area, authentic leadership focus on how true they and their leadership style are to their personal values and morals. Does the leader walk the walk or just talk the talk?

The second developing area, spiritual leadership, is also tied to values. Here the leader uses values and a sense of calling, or membership, to motivate the team.

The third developing area has the leader in the role of the servant. As a servant, the leader uses concepts like caring principles to focus on the followers' needs. These caring principles are wide ranging, and can be demonstrated as either traits (such as courage, humility) or behaviors (serving and developing others). A potential benefit here is that the team members become autonomous, knowledgeable, and servants themselves.

The fourth developing area, adaptive leadership, is the process whereby leaders encourage team members to adapt when confronting and solving problems and challenges, as well as facing and adapting to changes.

The fifth developing area, followership leadership, focuses on the team members and the role each plays in the leadership space.

Finally, the sixth developing area, discursive leadership, is based on the concept that leadership is not achieved through any specific traits, skills, or behaviors, but through communication negotiated with team members.

Categories of leadership	Developing areas of leadership
Do as a leader wishes	Authentic
Influence	Spiritual
Traits	Servant
Transformation	Adaptive
	Followership
	Discursive

Table 1.1. Northouse's Categories and Developing Areas of Leadership

The categories of leadership and developing areas of leadership as defined by Northouse are summarized in Table 1.1.

A Focus on Authentic Leadership

Each of the four leadership categories and six developing areas are covered in much more detail in Northouse's textbook. The concept of values-based leadership, however, which is a cornerstone of this book and the LeadershipWWEB podcast series, is most closely related to the first developing area, authentic leadership.

People want authentic leaders, Northouse points out, because authentic leaders can be trusted and thus willingly followed, since their motivations are honest and good—in other words, because their leadership is based on values that produce trust.

There are three different perspectives of authentic leadership: intrapersonal, interpersonal, and developmental. The intrapersonal perspective focuses on what goes on inside the leader—the leader's self-knowledge, self-regulation, and self-concept. On the other hand, the interpersonal perspective focuses more on the relational, interactional, and reciprocal nature of the leader, and what occurs between the leader and the team. The third perspective, developmental, is related to how authentic leadership needs to be nurtured in a leader.

We intentionally did not provide guidance to the podcast guests on intrapersonal, interpersonal, or developmental perspectives, and our discussions ended up being a blend of the three definitions. This allows listeners of the podcast and readers of this book to develop their own leadership framework based on what they learn during the discussions.

Perspectives of authentic leadership	Dimensions of authentic leadership
Intrapersonal	Passion
Interpersonal	Behavior
Developmental	Connectedness
	Consistency
	Compassion

Table 1.2. Northouse's Perspectives and Dimensions of Authentic Leadership (2018)

There is a very practical component to authentic leadership. It stems from the desires to serve others, know yourself, and know and lead from core values. If leaders cannot immediately cite examples of how they have held to their core values, they are not following such values, and what they call their core values are nothing more than a work of fiction.

Malik Sadiq, chief operating officer at LIVEKINDLY Collective (formerly senior vice president for global sourcing and business optimization at Tyson Foods), says leaders are owners of what they do. In the draft of a book he's working on (tentatively titled "We Love Math, Now Let's Lead"), Malik says leaders "accomplish results on their own because they are internally motivated to do so." You are not internally motivated unless you are authentic, and authentic leaders are defined by their core values.

Authentic leadership, according to Northouse, can be viewed through five dimensions: passion, behavior, connectedness, consistency, and compassion. Passion provides a strong sense of purpose, while behavior drives the strong values related to the right thing to do. This leads to connectedness, which establishes trusting relationships between individuals and groups. That in turn leads to consistency, where self-discipline is demonstrated and people act on their values. Finally, all four of these dimensions lead to compassion, which makes both the leader and the team sensitive to the plight of others. The perspectives of authentic leadership and dimensions of authentic leadership as defined by Northouse are summarized in Table 1.2.

The concept of allowing your values to guide you was also discussed by James Kouzes and Barry Posner. In *The Student Leadership Challenge* (2014), Kouzes and Posner emphasized that values influence all facets of people's lives, from personal goals to commitments, and from moral judgments to your behavior in various situations. In a sense, the authors equate values to bumper bowling: the values act as the bumpers and ensure that you stay within your lane as you make large and small, and conscious and subconscious, decisions every day.

A Theoretical Perspective

In addition to the practical component, there is a theoretical aspect to authentic leadership that breaks it into two stages. The first stage is a critical life event or a string of such events. These events feed the foundation of authentic leadership with positive psychological capacities and moral reasoning. The second stage is a lifelong process, but this process is catalyzed by critical life events.

The critical life events lead to better and stronger psychological capacities, moral reasoning, self-awareness, moral perspective, balanced processing, sage advice, and relational transparency. The four components in stage two lead to robust authentic leadership. Both the practical and theoretical perspectives can be influenced by confidence, hope, optimism, and resilience.

There are many strengths of authentic leadership. It fulfills the expressed need for trustworthy leadership in society and provides broad guidelines for those who want to become authentic leaders themselves. Authentic leadership also has an explicit moral dimension, which means it can be developed over time. Finally, authentic leadership can be quantified (something that every engineer loves) using the Authentic Leadership Questionnaire (ALQ) of Fred Walumbwa and coauthors (2008).

Authentic leadership was also discussed extensively by Susan Komives, Nance Lucas, and Timothy McMahon in *Exploring Leadership* (2013). These authors look at authentic leadership through the lens of reciprocal leadership and postindustrial leadership. They equate authentic leadership through two primary frameworks:

- The base of all positive, socially constructive forms of leadership
- The junction of positive psychology, transformational leadership, and moral or ethical leadership

In addition, leaders who practice authentic leadership share many dimensions. For example,

- They are confident, hopeful, optimistic, resilient, transparent, moral, ethical, and future-oriented.

- They give priority to developing others to be leaders.
- They know who they are, what they believe, and what they value, and just as importantly, they act transparently on their beliefs and values.
- They act to build credibility, win the respect and trust of others, and encourage diverse viewpoints and the building of networks of collaborative relationships with followers.
- They do not fake their leadership.
- They do not take on a leadership role for status, honor, or other personal rewards.

The similarities between how Northouse and authors such as Komives, Lucas, and McMahon discuss authentic leadership are obvious, but it is useful to see many of the same things through slightly different lenses. The exercise of looking at the same topic in slightly different ways drives home the key theoretical perspectives of authentic leadership.

Challenges of Authentic Leadership

There also are some challenges facing the theory of authentic leadership. For instance, the academic theory of authentic leadership is still in development, so many of the concepts are not fully substantiated. This is partially because authentic leadership has a weak empirical-based foundation, and the academic theory has not been tested for validity.

In addition, the moral component of authentic leadership is not fully explained. How are a leader's values related to that person's self-awareness? It is well established that people are drawn toward people who know who they are and what they are about. Wendy Wagner and Daniel Ostick, who wrote the workbook to go with *Exploring Leadership*, show how self-awareness can be developed and nurtured through "personal visioning reflection" (2013). This reflection revolves around asking key questions such as:

- What are your top five core values?
- Based on stories from your past, what are some of your strengths?
- If you had to write a personal vision statement, what would you write?

These questions drive to the heart of self-awareness, but they also bring up more questions about values and authentic leadership. What path is

Dimensions	Practical perspectives	Theoretical perspectives	Influences	Challenges ahead
Passion	Desire to serve others	Psychological capacities	Confidence	Weak empirical-based foundation
Behavior	Know themselves	Moral reasoning	Hope	Incomplete moral component
Connectedness	Lead from core values	Self-awareness	Optimism	Fuzzy boundaries
Consistency		Moral perspective	Resilience	Younger generations
Compassion		Balanced processing		
		Sage advice		
		Relational transparency		

Table 1.3. Breaking Down Authentic Leadership → Tying to LeadershipWWEB

followed (or what process occurs) when moral values affect other components of leadership? How does authentic leadership result in positive organization outcomes? These types of questions show just how much more can be examined within the realm of authentic leadership.

In fact, the boundaries of authentic leadership are not clear, which is another challenge facing the theory. One such boundary is whether psychological capacities should be included as a component of authentic leadership. If they are included, there is a strong possibility that the construct of authentic leadership could become too broad, which would make it difficult to measure.

Finally, it is not known whether younger generations can be effectively led by authentic leaders. For example, one of the current younger generations, millennials, tend to have a high level of individualism and a much stronger commitment to work-life balance than their predecessors do. The impact of those two traits, along with millennials' preference for extrinsic rewards, creates large unknowns across the multiple generations in today's workforce.

Table 1.3 will be an anchor for the rest of the book. The dimensions, practical perspectives, theoretical perspectives, influences, and challenges ahead listed in Table 1.3 will be referenced and discussed in each chapter.

Therefore, all of the opportunities of leadership will be specifically linked to Table 1.3. If the concepts in Table 1.3 are directly related to an opportunity of leadership, a check mark will be beside the concept within the table. Each chapter will have this table, and will allow for quick reference to see how each opportunity of leadership links to the different facets of authentic leadership as summarized in Table 1.3.

While we won't know for sure until authentic leadership is put into practice for a few more years, we believe that authentic leadership will only grow in use over the years and that it will be accepted as a legitimate and successful form of leadership. The discussions with our podcast guests only reinforced this belief.

Twists and Turns

Angela Grayson's value of ethical kept tugging at the back of our minds as we went about writing this book, largely because values are the base of how individuals act ethically. She specifically said that it was important to "be ethical, always."

Angela is the principal member and founder of Precipice IP, a law firm that specializes in helping technology and science start-ups, and she has degrees in chemistry, physical chemistry, and law. She learned about ethics as a child, the importance of ethics has been reinforced in almost every step of her life, and she thinks about being ethical as she goes through each day.

It was only natural that she brought up ethics as an absolute value when she was a guest on our LeadershipWWEB podcast series. And it's also only natural that ethics became a defining thread that is woven throughout this book. After all, the concept of being ethical is critical whether people are watching or you are alone, whether you are the leader or are working with the leaders around you, and in every other facet of leadership. Furthermore, it is often said that integrity is tested when no one is looking. We believe that in this context, ethics and integrity can be used interchangeably.

There is no one way to practice or execute leadership. There is no list to follow to have success. There is no single goal of leadership. Instead, leadership is a journey. And in all leadership journeys, there are inevitably unexpected twists and turns.

For instance, originally we were going to center this book on values-based leadership. As the journey continued, however, we found a lot of overlap between that topic and authentic leadership. Therefore, we decided to frame the chapters around opportunities, and both authentic leadership and values would form the content of each chapter. While some values aren't discussed at all in some chapters, the value of integrity (or ethics, the term Grayson preferred) proved relevant to every discussion.

All the insights and examples from our podcast guests had at least one other thing in common: they were pure gold to anyone who wants to understand and practice values-based, authentic leadership. Whether you are just starting your lifelong journey as a student of leadership or you have been on this path for decades, we feel confident you'll find as much value in reading about these nuggets as we found in writing about them.

Key Takeaways

- The four main categories of leadership are: (1) do as a leader wishes, (2) influence, (3) traits, and (4) transformation.
- The six developing areas of leadership are: (1) authentic, (2) spiritual, (3) servant, (4) adaptive, (5) followership, and (6) discursive.
- The three perspectives of authentic leadership are: (1) intrapersonal, (2) interpersonal, and (3) developmental.
- Authentic leadership creates a bridge to values-based leadership through the five dimensions, the three practical perspectives, the seven theoretical perspectives, and the four influences of authentic leadership.

Value	Podcast
Be ethical, always	Angela Grayson
Leadership	Chris McCoy
Integrity	Sam Alley, Troy Alley, Mike Duke, Mike Johnson, Kim LaScola Needy, Pam McGinnis, Mario Ramirez, Shelley Simpson, Donnie Smith, and John White

Table 1.4. Values Discussed in This Chapter

CHAPTER 2

Of Myths and Mentoring

Points to Ponder

- What is the meaning of mentoring?
- What is the difference between formal and informal mentoring?
- Why do you need a formal mentor, not just informal mentors?
- Why is it more important to have mentors as you advance in authority and responsibility?
- What are the dimensions of good mentors?

The concept of mentoring dates back to the origins of humanity, with forms of it being practiced in cultures all around the globe. Spiritual leaders would take on disciples, teachers would take on pupils, trade workers would take on apprentices, knights would take on pages, and so on—all in an effort to train the next generation of workers and leaders.

While there are all sorts of related terms and plenty of overlap with concepts like discipleship, coaching, consulting, and advising, the term *mentoring* originates in Greek mythology. Odysseus, the king of Ithaca, was leaving for what he knew would be an extended period to do battle at Troy, so he put a friend in charge of his home, including the education of his son, Telemachus. That friend's name was Mentor. Centuries later, someone who fills the roles of teacher, coach, protector, counselor, and guide is known as a mentor.

We take a pretty open-ended approach to defining a mentorship. We see it as a voluntary but intentional relationship with a focus on supporting another person's long-term growth and development. We do not see it as one-directional. Although one of the participants often has more experience than the other, the relationship and learning goes in both directions. Within that context, mentoring can be personal, professional, or some combination of the two.

In any case, a mentor is more like a library you visit in search of insights than a GPS that gives you specific directions. Mentors offer wisdom, guidance, support, and recommendations. They challenge you to figure out your destination and make a plan for the journey, but they don't make decisions for you. They teach by example and by asking the right questions rather than by giving lectures or detailed instructions. These concepts all fall under the umbrella of sage advice, which is one of the theoretical perspectives of authentic leadership.

Jessica Hendrix, Scott Bennett, and Greg Brown all emphasized the importance of learning when they were guests on the WWEB podcast. Some of them talked about learning from others, and some of them discussed learning from problem solving. Even during the process of learning from problem solving, it is helpful to seek your mentor's wisdom because this will help you both solve the problem and learn more about how to solve problems in general.

Jess tied learning to problem solving and teaching. She believes everyone should always be learning, not only from books and podcasts but also from one another. People who are constantly trying to learn from others provide tangible evidence that they value the people who are teaching them something new.

Jess shared a wonderful story about how this can be tied to mentoring. When she was working with one of her employees, she felt like she had a crystal ball. She knew exactly what the employee had to do, but she realized she had two choices: tell the employee the outcome and prevent any failure or let the employee choose the path and learn from any mistakes.

Jess chose the latter option. She knew failure provides some of the most powerful teaching moments if the person who failed is mentored correctly. Jess believes leaders should expect failure, and the important thing is how you fail and how you adjust moving forward. On the other side of the relationship, the employee Jess was mentoring gained valuable experience, which demonstrates the power of having a mentor. This will be discussed further in chapter 6.

Is There Just One Way to Be Mentored?

A variety of models for mentoring in business environments have evolved through the years, and there is no one right way to make mentorships work. They can vary, for instance, across a spectrum from informal to formal. At one end of the spectrum, you simply observe people around you and try to learn from what you see and hear. At the other end, you and a mentor have an explicit agreement to participate in a relationship with defined roles and expectations.

Working in a team provides frequent learning opportunities from a number of informal mentors. You can learn from everyone in the group, including those you don't want to emulate. The key is to listen with a learning mind-set, noticing how others on the team respond to each other and how they lead, follow, encourage, learn, and teach. Then open yourself to their feedback about your performance as a team member.

Find someone you think will give honest, relevant feedback and ask for their opinions on how you are doing and how you can improve. When you don't like what you hear, do not defend yourself. Instead, repeat what you think you heard and ask if you are correct. If you offend someone on your team, meet with them to find out why you offended them. Listen, repeat what you think you heard and ask if you are correct, and apologize. This is a way to turn a team into a group of informal mentors.

Mike Duke, the former CEO of Walmart, told us he learned one of his most important leadership lessons about integrity from an informal mentorship. When Mike was working in Atlanta for a retailer, his boss, John Weitnauer, typically mentored by example rather than in a prescribed fashion. One day Weitnauer was trying to purchase petroleum, but this was the early 1970s when many suppliers were bone dry. A representative for one supplier, however, offered to send a shipment the next day—if Weitnauer would send along a high-end tennis racket as a personal gift for the representative.

Instead of signing off on the purchase, Weitnauer told the representative he wasn't interested in the gas. Then he said he wanted to speak to the man's supervisor within the hour to discuss how the company was going to change its ethics and standards, as the purchase of petroleum should not be tied to a bribe. Weitnauer sent a very clear message, Mike recalled, on what was the right way to do business and on the fact that there was never a time to compromise on ethical standards.

Authentic leadership can and should involve mentorships all along the formality spectrum. The more formal, however, are particularly valuable because those proactively address all three perspectives of authentic leadership—intrapersonal, interpersonal, and developmental—in the most direct, intentional, and effective ways.

Formal mentoring relationships add deeper insights and levels of accountability that help ensure growth is taking place, especially in areas where leaders might not even realize it's needed. An informal mentor might not even know that he or she is a mentor and therefore might not say something that needs to be said. A formal mentor, on the other hand, feels a sense of obligation to identify and speak to the most relevant issues you face.

If you want to lead with integrity, for example, you need at least one formal mentor who helps you detect blind spots in your decisions and comments that may lack—or be perceived to lack—integrity.

Most leaders, of course, value integrity. As Mike told us, integrity is the foundation for all other values. Almost half of the people we interviewed said integrity is one of their core values. The concept of leading from core values is a practical perspective of authentic leadership, which could indicates that integrity is an example of a practical perspective of authentic leadership. While others didn't include integrity as a stated value, this may have been only because they saw it as a necessary condition for successful leadership. No one we interviewed said integrity was not important to good leadership.

While it is easy to espouse integrity as an important value, however, it's not always easy to live up to it. Leaders are seldom presented with scenarios like case studies in which they know from the get-go that they need to consciously factor in integrity and the choices between right and wrong, or good and evil, are clear. More often, today's leaders make quick decisions in high-pressure situations in which the issues of integrity at first seem small and insignificant but later snowball into an avalanche of complexity.

That's why it's essential to have at least one formal mentor who is willing to tell you when there is a contradiction between your desire to lead with integrity and what others hear in your words and see in your actions. It takes time and commitment to develop that level of trust and transparency, but it is worthwhile if you really want to lead with integrity. The component of transparency is especially important since relational transparency is one of the theoretical perspectives of authentic leadership.

Who Needs Mentors?

Every stage of a leader's journey brings new expectations and challenges, and discernment doesn't always come naturally. While experience is a master teacher, leaders also need to lean into the wisdom of others, regardless of where they are on the organizational flowchart. So whether you are a CEO or just starting out, you need mentors who can guide you. In fact, mentors are not necessarily people who outrank you, but they should have principles you need to learn and put into practice.

The University of Arkansas bakes mentorships into many of its programs and much of its curriculum, so that students are exposed to the benefits of the experience as a complement to their traditional education. For instance, the MBA program in the Sam M. Walton College of Business provides all students with corporate mentors who meet with them monthly, and a committee of the program's alumni also provides mentors who are on call to respond to issues students are facing.

The college also created the Executive Engagement Marketplace, a searchable listing of industry practitioners available on its intranet that helps faculty find guest speakers for classes; companies willing to host a class or group for a visit; and leaders and companies willing to provide mentoring, business coaching, résumé coaching, and research participants, as well as to conduct mock interviews. And working through the Brewer Family Entrepreneurship Hub on the square in Fayetteville, the college connects professional mentors with student teams who are working on projects (connectedness is one of the dimensions of authentic leadership).

The vision and mission behind the searchable listing created by the Walton College highlights many of the values that the LeadershipWWEB podcast guests discussed, including entrepreneurship. Angela Grayson, for instance, had a background in chemistry before earning her law degree and founding Precipice IP, a strategic technology law services firm. Angela, who now spends most of her time on patent law, said one of the things she enjoys most is working with different entrepreneurs and hearing their stories. It motivates her, she said, and increases her passion (another dimension of authentic leadership).

A key moment in Angela's journey came when she was being mentored as a graduate student at the University of Mississippi, before she went to law school. She had a professor who had been trained at Harvard University and the University of California, Berkeley and whose standards were sky-high. This professor did not make any excuses or say "I can't do it." Angela felt the standards were outrageous, but she studied hard and the professor encouraged her. And the more Angela lived up to those high expectations, the more her confidence grew. That experience as a student became a launching pad into her legal career, and hard work and high expectations are now foundations of her philosophy.

It's not just students or young professionals, however, who need mentors. The Walton College is also creating a mentorship program specifically for faculty and staff who face challenges in areas related to diversity, equity, and inclusion. And as students become leaders in the workforce, they need mentoring that grows with them throughout their careers.

In fact, the need for a mentor typically grows as a leader's responsibilities increase. There are at least two reasons for this.

First, as responsibilities in leadership increase, meeting them consumes more and more of a leader's time and energy (and technical contributions become less time-consuming). Since leaders at upper levels deal with high levels of uncertainty, no one leader will have all the answers, and therefore, these leaders will have a greater need than those at lower levels for the insights and perspectives of mentors.

Second, as leaders advance in an organization, they tend to become more insulated from criticism and more likely to face temptations that come with the trappings of their role. High-level leaders typically are shown deference because of their title, their past successes, and the simple fact that they have things like a nice office, a big salary, and a reserved parking spot. They are questioned less often by those around them, not because they are always right but because they are seen as the boss. If they aren't careful and proactive, it's easy for them to act as if they have the market cornered on the right answers to every situation. Arrogance often sets in slowly and builds without leaders even realizing it's there. Mentors help these leaders see their blind spots so they can lead with an open mind and a humble heart.

Dimensions	Practical perspectives	Theoretical perspectives	Influences
Passion✔	Desire to serve others	Psychological capacities	Confidence✔
Behavior✔	Know themselves✔	Moral reasoning✔	Hope
Connectedness✔	Lead from core values✔	Self-awareness✔	Optimism
Consistency		Moral perspective✔	Resilience
Compassion		Balanced processing✔	
		Sage advice✔	
		Relational transparency✔	

Table 2.1. Breaking Down Authentic Leadership → Tying to Mentoring

✔ indicates a direct relationship to an opportunity of leadership.

Many of the most recognized high-level leaders provide testimony to the value of having a mentor regardless of how much success they've achieved. For instance, David Nish was promoted from CFO to CEO at Standard Life in 2010 and sought out Niall FitzGerald, a former chairman of Unilever, as a mentor (de Janasz and Peiperl 2015). Warren Buffett mentored Bill Gates. Bernard Levin mentored Arianna Huffington. And Maya Angelou mentored Oprah Winfrey (Smyth 2017).

The *Harvard Business Review* published a study in April 2015 that highlighted the power of mentoring. Of the forty-five CEOs in the survey who had formal mentoring arrangements, 84 percent said mentors had helped them avoid expensive mistakes and more quickly become proficient in their roles. And 71 percent felt "certain" that having a mentor had improved their company's performance (de Janasz and Peiperl 2015).

It's hard for me (Matt) to understate the value mentoring has added to the results of my work as dean of the Walton College. In addition to the input I get from my team, I count on a number of formal and informal advisors who shape my leadership and decisions. The informal advisors include my family, students, business leaders, academics and administrators at other universities, and just about anyone else who speaks into my life. My formal advisors include individual mentors, my Dean's Alumni Advisory Council, my Dean's Executive Advisory Board, and my Dean's Roundtable of Entrepreneurs and Market Makers.

Finding a Mentor

Advisory boards and informal mentoring typically are untimed adventures: leaders participate in them all the time regardless of the circumstances. Formal mentoring, on the other hand, often results from a specific need. What are some signs that indicate you might have such a need?

One common thread is change: you've been promoted to a new role; you want to be promoted to a new role; there's been a significant change in your work world, like a new company strategy; or you've been assigned a key project with tight deadlines.

Those types of change come with signals that indicate you could use some outside wisdom and perspective as you navigate the related uncertainty. You might have feelings of stress and anxiety because of the pressure that comes with your work. You might have difficulty articulating the direction you and your team need to take because of the uncertainty about which path to take. You might feel the weight of mounting questions and decisions that loom on the horizon. You might feel overwhelmed by all the different opportunities available to you and your team. Or you might sense a growing ambition for some achievement that would stretch you beyond what you've ever done.

Once you've decided you need a formal mentoring relationship, you can't just pick anyone as your mentor. You need the right mentor. That person might be a coworker, but he or she also might work in a totally different industry or be retired. The key to finding the right mentor is to scan your world for options, talk to people you trust, and then vet the people you think might work well in your situation.

When I (John) was head of the Department of Industrial Engineering at the University of Arkansas, I had one mentor who advised me on many of my steps. The same was true when I was dean of engineering at two universities, Kansas State University and University of Arkansas. In each case, the selection of a mentor was natural and clear. The person's morals, ethics, life priorities, and work-life balance to a tee. He was the type of leader I dreamed of being, and I needed him more as my responsibilities increased.

The importance of aligning with your mentor on morals cannot be overlooked, as moral reasoning and moral perspective are both theoretical perspectives of authentic leadership.

In some cases, a mentor might be recommended by your supervisor or human resources team, or as a part of a leadership or executive education program. More often, however, the mentor is someone you identify and approach on your own. A good place to start is by asking the person to have coffee with you and seeking their input on something that's going on in your life or work. If that discussion goes well, you simply ask if they would be willing to meet regularly in a more formal way. If they say no, thank them for not committing to something they weren't able to do and then look for someone else.

How will you know if a person would be a good mentor?

Perhaps the most important criterion is that you and the person have compatible values. Some differences of opinions and perspectives are extremely valuable in a mentoring relationship, but if your core beliefs stand in opposition to each other, then the mentorship probably won't work well. Work-life balance is a prime example. Perhaps you see achieving it as a high priority, but you struggle to keep work from creeping into family time. If a potential mentor works eighty hours a week and doesn't remember the names of his children, he might not be a great fit. The idea of balance, whether between work and life or in other areas, is one of the theoretical perspectives of authentic leadership.

If you have a specific issue that you want to focus on with a mentor, then you'll want to factor that into the equation. For instance, if you want to launch a new company, then it makes sense to find a mentor with experience as an entrepreneur. Or you may be running a company that has grown to the point where you need a better understanding of managing the more complex financial aspects of a big business. In that case, you want someone who has been there and done that.

Even if you aren't in need of a mentor for a specific reason, it's wise to always keep searching for potential mentors. As mentioned in the introduction, I (Andrew) never expected to find a mentor in a spin class, yet because Matt and I took advantage of that opportunity, a mentoring relationship began that was outside of any of the formal mechanisms at the University of Arkansas.

Regardless of the specific focus of your mentorship, it takes time to be sure if a mentor is the right fit. But there are some things to look for during that first meeting and over the course of the first few months of meeting that might follow. Here are key characteristics you should look for in a good mentor (Lawrence et al. 2019).

Good mentors understand you. You want mentors who listen, can relate to your feelings, communicate in conversation, and get your logic even if they don't always agree with it.

Good mentors believe in you. You want mentors who see your potential and care about your success, as a person and a professional. They see the relationship as a worthy investment of their time and energy.

Good mentors help you move forward. You want mentors who ask the right questions, draw out insights, and help you sort through your challenges. They collaborate with you to help you see your weaknesses and blind spots as sources of potential growth.

Good mentors create accountability. Good mentors don't allow your promises to die on the vine. They hold you accountable with conversations that aren't always easy but that are soaked in truth, are straightforward, and have your best interest at heart.

Good mentors build trust. You want mentors who keep your conversations confidential, of course, but who also earn trust by delivering results. The more they ask well-timed questions that cause you to have aha moments, the more you will trust the advice, direction, and insights they provide.

Good mentors grow with you. A good mentoring relationship is a rising tide that lifts both boats. Good mentors are humble enough to see their own need for growth, and they will use the relationship to change in areas that are important to them.

Your role, of course, is to do the hard work of being a sponge. To get something out of the relationship, you have to invest in it. You have to collaborate with your mentor on the expectations, be vulnerable about your weakness, meet criticism with a thick skin, ask good questions, listen to learn, take good notes, do your homework, put what you are learning into practice by focusing on your behavior (one of the dimensions of authentic leadership), more specifically, change your behavior, and show gratitude for the relationship and its results.

If you aren't willing to work hard and get out of your comfort zone, the best mentor in the world won't do you much good. I (John) remember one critical input by my number one mentor. I was under the gun, being criticized heavily and taking it hard. My mentor looked at me and said, "You may not be tough enough for this job." That spoke volumes. It was a direct hit on my role as a leader. From then on, my skin was thicker.

While relationships forged during a mentorship often last a long time, the formal aspect of mentoring typically runs its course at some point, usually because you accomplish your goals or because your circumstances and needs change. If it becomes difficult to find things to discuss or if the mentor frequently misses meetings, it's probably time to end the formal relationship.

Reflections on Finding a Good Mentor

The key characteristics to look for in a good mentor include several of the top values that the LeadershipWWEB podcast guests discussed, including accountability and confidence.

For instance, Pam McGinnis, president of global marketing at Phillips 66, told us that whatever the assignment, project, timeline, or topic of discussion, you need to own it and be accountable. Pam recognizes that mistakes happen when people are moving forward aggressively, so she has no problem with someone making a mistake—unless that person repeatedly makes the same mistake. And if you do make a mistake, she expects you to own it.

Owning mistakes, making amends, and apologizing will create trust. Trying to sweep something under the rug always creates more problems. And problems that aren't confronted and owned will only become worse over time.

Pam recalled one time when she experienced the importance and effectiveness of accountability. She and her team were working on a project, and she felt like she was asking one of her direct reports the same questions over and over again. Finally, Pam lost it and threw a tantrum.

"Why am you not getting this?" she yelled. "I am tired of complaining!"

The person responded by saying, "It feels like you are attacking me."

Pam reflected on the exchange for the rest of the day and into the evening. The first thing she did the next day was to go to the office of the direct report and apologize. She acknowledged that she was frustrated but admitted that she should not have thrown the tantrum. By apologizing, Pam demonstrated her accountability to the people working for her. It also demonstrated humility. After the conversation, while the typical challenges of a work environment continued, Pam felt that she and the direct report had a much stronger relationship.

Whether we are interacting with a supervisor, a peer, or anyone else, Pam told us, we all need to treat other people with respect, and if we fall short, we need to hold ourselves accountable. This calls for a high level of goodwill, but that is exactly what is necessary for everyone to thrive. In a mentoring relationship, this is a message that is critical not only to talk about but also to act out.

In addition to accountability, another key characteristic to look for in a good mentor is that they need to believe in you, which can help the mentor build confidence in you. Troy Alley, the executive vice president and chief operating officer of Con-Real, talked about the importance of a mentor's confidence. Confidence is not only one of Troy's values, but it is also one of the influences of authentic leadership. Troy said he learned this from his mother, who instilled a high level of confidence in him and his siblings.

Troy compared confidence to climbing a mountain. You can always look back and see your progress, and this progress gives you the confidence to continue. The beauty of confidence is that it is contagious. As you build confidence, so will the team around you.

Confidence, Troy explained, is both internal and external. You should never lose confidence in what you can do, he said, because everyone has a certain amount of talent and intelligence. This is a part of internal confidence. It is necessary for people to know themselves to have this internal confidence. The concept of knowing yourself is a practical perspective of authentic leadership, and the concept of self-awareness is a theoretical perspective of authentic leadership.

It is important, however, to maintain that inner confidence in all of your actions, which is the external portion of confidence. One of Troy's largest challenges, for instance, involved going to the University of Arkansas in 1965. Not only was he working his way through the challenging electrical engineering curriculum, but he was one of the few Blacks on campus at the time. He also came from very humble beginnings. He turned to his two c's: confidence and commitment. This shows another layer of confidence as you need both internal and external confidence, in addition to the continued confidence of your mentor. His mother continued to support him. His strong upbringing had taught him that once he determined he could do something, he had to follow through, and he did so by earning a degree in electrical engineering.

Key Takeaways

- Mentoring doesn't always provide precise instructions; it often is more like a library of information you can refer to when needed.
- Good mentors allow you to make mistakes—as long as you learn from them.
- The best mentors have high levels of integrity in all facets of their personal and professional lives.
- Whether you are an intern at an engineering firm or the CEO of a Fortune 500 company, the value of mentorship is priceless. In fact, mentors typically are more valuable as your responsibilities increase, because there are more gray areas and decisions are not as straightforward.
- When picking a mentor, look for someone who understands you, believes in you, helps you move forward, creates accountability, builds trust, and grows with you.
- Do not be discouraged if your first mentor (or two) is not quite what you were looking for. Keep your eyes open, broaden your search, and you will find a high-quality mentor.

Value	Podcast
Integrity	Sam Alley, Troy Alley, Mike Duke, Mike Johnson, Kim LaScola Needy, Pam McGinnis, Mario Ramirez, Shelley Simpson, Donnie Smith, and John White
Accountability	J. R. Jones and Pam McGinnis
Work ethic	Greg Brown, Angela Grayson, Pam McGinnis, and Shelley Simpson
Learning	Scott Bennett, Greg Brown, and Jessica Hendrix
Confidence	Mario Ramirez and Troy Alley

Table 2.2. Values Discussed in This Chapter

CHAPTER 3

Being a Team Player

Points to Ponder

- What are the benefits of working on a team versus working as an individual?
- Why is inclusiveness important when working in a group?
- How do communication and group work go hand in hand?
- How is emotional intelligence related to being in a group?
- What are the nine dimensions of an effective team?

Whether you graduated forty years ago or ten years ago, or you are still in school, you are bound to remember a time when you seemingly did all the work in a group while your teammates did very little besides reap the benefits of your efforts.

Those types of experiences often make people want to slip off to a distant corner and work by themselves, eliminating any personal discomfort or risk. Pursuing this route, however, goes against research that shows the benefits of working in a group are greater than those of working as an individual.

For instance, Marco Casari, Jingjing Zhang, and Christine Jackson used the Winner's Curse game to compare individual and group performance. In the game, one party attempts to buy a company from a second party. The buyer needs to make a take-it-or-leave-it offer, and the seller needs to accept or decline. Of course, the seller has more accurate information than the buyer does, because the seller owns the company.

The researchers found that individuals rarely placed optimal bids. In addition, individuals who acquired a company incurred losses and did not correct their behaviors over time. On the other hand, a group operating as the buyer was more likely than an individual buyer to place an optimal bid and correct its behaviors over time (Casari et al. 2012).

Another benefit to working in groups is that collaboration exposes you to people with backgrounds and experiences that are differ from yours—not just when it comes to gender and race, but also in terms of socio-economic status, age, ability or disability, and education level.

Chris McCoy, the former vice-chancellor for finance and administration at the University of Arkansas, told us that leaders risk missing out on opportunities for success by not including multiple frames of reference in their decisions. Diversity within a group enriches the entire group. Therefore, when we are solving problems, we need to work with people who complement us and who bring multiple perspectives to bear on the problem. This leads to more effective productivity and better problem solving.

The term *effective* is interesting, especially in the context of a group setting. In *The Contrarian's Guide to Leadership*, Steven Sample (2003), the former president of the University of Southern California, points out that being effective requires a clear yet compelling vision while inspiring trust, commitment, and self-sacrifice in those around you. When group members are effective, they keep an eye on the goal while pushing themselves and the entire group relentlessly.

In contrast, the concept of *good* is a function of moral values. Facing up to moral choices is the essence of good leadership, and it also can be an effective part of working in a team. There are questions you should ask yourself privately when working in a group that can aid in your decision making. These questions include:

- How much ground can I yield and still be true to my moral core?
- How far can I be pushed before I need to walk away from my duties?
- What hill (the hill can be a situation, decision, solution, and so on) will I never retreat from? What hill am I willing to sacrifice everything for?
- How are decisions sorted into legal versus ethical?

The lines between moral behavior and ethical behavior certainly have gray areas, but one way Sample defined moral behavior was as actions that you are willing to take on another's behalf when no one is checking on you. While working in a group, it is important to develop and follow your own moral convictions while being as open as possible to the strongly held moral beliefs of others.

Moral reasoning and moral perspective are two of the theoretical perspectives of authentic leadership. When working in a group, channeling moral reasoning and perspective as an individual allows the group to benefit from the strong personal foundation that you have built for yourself.

Since moral reasoning and moral perspective are a part of your personal foundation, the practical perspective of "lead from core values" under authentic leadership also is demonstrated through teamwork, because we must stay true to our core. If you cannot cite examples of how your core values shape your actions, reactions, and leadership, then they are not core values.

Group Work and Inclusiveness

One of the best ways to effectively improve group dynamics, according to Pam McGinnis, president of global marketing at Phillips 66, is to create an environment where everyone feels like they belong—a feeling that is a cornerstone of diversity, equity, and inclusion.

Pam told us that when leaders work hard to create an inclusive culture, others tend to follow. When people in a group constantly feel like they are being lifted up, she said, inclusiveness grows like a snowball rolling down a hill. If a person in a group feels like she belongs, for example, she will be willing to share what she knows, be vulnerable, and take risks.

Pam spent a good bit of our conversation discussing the importance of being vulnerable. Leaders, she said, must be willing to ask what others might think of as a dumb question. Vulnerability also shows when leaders are creative in their problem-solving, come up with new ideas, and share ideas for innovation.

Those types of constructive actions will take place only if everyone in the group knows that it is safe to take risks, ask questions, accelerate creativity, develop ideas, and lead in innovation—all of which are critical to long-term success. If industry, the public sector, and academe continue to move toward making it safe to do these things, Pam believes that the results could transform how work is done and is one example of a leader purposely setting direction.

Everyone has their own background, baggage, and childhood, as well as other experiences that are specific to them. It is difficult, Pam acknowledged, for people in a group to make space for all of these backgrounds. But if they don't, group members can't be vulnerable, which means that they won't share new ideas, ask probing questions, or even admit that they may not know something. They will be reluctant to brainstorm about the wackiest ideas because they fear being made fun of.

Pam believes creating truly inclusive teams can give Phillips 66 a competitive advantage. If employees can bring their whole selves to work and are respected, heard, and valued, she said, then they will give 100 percent. Each employee, either as an individual or in a group, will be motivated, take on extra projects, and create better business results.

Many of the Chief Executive Officers (CEOs) we interviewed also discussed themes around diversity, equity, and inclusion, including Donnie Smith, the former CEO of Tyson Foods; Greg Brown, the chairman and CEO of Motorola Solutions; Mike Duke, the former CEO of Walmart; and Tony Vinciquerra, the chairman and CEO of Sony Pictures Entertainment (SPE). All of these CEOs talked about the power of diversity and how products became stronger with a diverse team.

These concepts played directly into Tony's values of transparency, openness, and inclusiveness. He has found that getting the majority of employees to buy into decisions allows them to "sing the same song from the same page." A key to this is including a wide range of employees. When that critical mass is reached and the majority is thinking along the same lines that you are thinking, the naysayers and disrupters will go underground.

The beauty of this system, said Tony, was that once everyone was going in the same direction, the leader can simply step out of the way. If top talent is recruited and high standards are expected and maintained, everyone will do their job at the high level.

Tony, however, is not naive. He recognizes that the hardest part is getting the endorsement of a majority of constituents. He knows that he will never get everyone to agree, but he uses techniques such as hour-long question-and-answer sessions with employees to make sure everyone has all the needed information. He is constantly amazed by the things that people think are true and the thought processes that take place.

By using the informal question-and-answer sessions, Tony can deliver a clear and concise message on the importance of inclusiveness on the many

Dimensions	Practical perspectives	Theoretical perspectives	Influences
Passion	Desire to serve others✔	Psychological capacities	Confidence
Behavior	Know themselves✔	Moral reasoning✔	Hope
Connectedness	Lead from core values✔	Self-awareness✔	Optimism✔
Consistency✔		Moral perspective✔	Resilience✔
Compassion✔		Balanced processing✔	
		Sage advice	
		Relational transparency✔	

Table 3.1. Breaking Down Authentic Leadership → Tying to Working in a Group

✔ indicates a direct relationship to an opportunity of leadership.

fronts within SPE. In addition, Tony listens, synthesizes, and can then move forward in a much more efficient and decisive manner.

Inclusiveness leads to decisiveness, a key part of Abraham Lincoln's approach to leadership. During Lincoln's presidency, the cabinet contained a diverse group of political rivals, including three men who had run against him for the Republican nomination. Members of his cabinet often disagreed with each other and with Lincoln, but he used those differences of opinion to drive decisive decision making during one of the most turbulent times in America's history.

Authentic leadership has many components of inclusiveness. For example, inclusiveness involves trying to understand others and build consensus, which are both ways in which you serve others. In addition, by purposely being inclusive, you are opening the door to relational transparency, which is a theoretical perspective of authentic leadership.

Group Work Requires Communication

Troy Alley, the executive vice president and chief operating officer of Con-Real, spent a good bit of his youth working with his father at the family's gas station in Pine Bluff, Arkansas, and he learned much more than how to check a car's oil level or tire pressure. Among many other things, he learned the importance of listening when living out the value of communication.

Troy believes communication is essential to everything leaders do. When he reflects on the three actions of a leader described in John Kotter's *Harvard Business Review* article "What Leaders Really Do" (1990)—set the direction, gain alignment, and provide motivation—he sees that all of them are anchored in communication. Business is about people (solving problems for and adding value to them), and that can't be done, he said, without effective communication.

At the heart of effective communication, Troy told us, is a giving mentality that results in listening to learn from others. Mark Goulston, the author of *Just Listen* (2015), says the same thing. He and Troy both advocate the concept of empathetic listening. That is, as you listen, you empathize in your mind to relate to what is being said and never try to add to the other person's story. In fact, being an empathetic listener is fun and brings a deeper understanding of the situation at hand.

Troy told us that he continually seeks opportunities to listen, and that he pays attention not just with his ears but also with his eyes—as well as showing with the rest of his body that he is listening. All of this helps him communicate that he is empathizing and trying to understand your perspective.

Communication is one of the most important methods of both solving problems for and adding value to people. Troy pointed out that each member of a group may have a unique perspective, a unique problem, and something different in mind. The multiplicity of perspectives, problems, and mind-sets is confounded by the fact that people may not be able to clearly articulate their messages and, therefore, other group members may need to read between the lines and empathize.

When Troy was in college, for instance, he listened to his roommate enough to know that he loved to play the stereo until he went to bed. One night in particular, Troy needed to study and didn't want to listen to the music, so he didn't return to his room until 10:30 p.m., just to avoid any potential conflict and to accommodate his roommate's preferences. At the end of a long day, Troy said, you may not want to hear complaints, opinions you disagree with, or requests that challenge you to accommodate others.

But, he added, it is important to recognize that everyone has had a hard day, and the simple act of listening can help make the situation better.

The concept of listening is also developed in *The Contrarian's Guide to Leadership*, where Sample discusses the importance of acquiring new ideas and gathering and assessing information without rushing to judgment. He then discusses the fact that people need to look through the eyes of others while also seeing the same issue or challenge through their own unique perspective. This can be done by not only actively listening, but also by asking relevant and probing questions.

An important component to active listening is the ability to absorb stories (that is, to be an empathetic listener), reports, complaints, posturings, accusations, extravagant claims, and prejudices without immediately offering a defined response.

Group Work Requires Decisiveness

We briefly touched on decisiveness above, but it warrants a closer examination. In addition to communication, another key to active listening is knowing when to stop and make a decision so that the organization can move forward.

In *Lincoln on Leadership*, Donald Phillips (1992) devotes a chapter to the decisiveness of leaders, which can easily be translated into making decisions in a group setting. One of the first concepts Phillips discusses is that people should not squabble about small issues; instead, they should trust the group to move in the right direction. By moving beyond a focus on small issues, multiple objectives—no matter what the size—can be achieved with one action. Not only is this an efficient use of time, but it will ensure that the group is moving forward in a consistent and coherent direction.

One way to trust the group to move in the right direction is to use each individual's strength. If someone in your group does a certain task well or has a specific talent, let them do that task or make use of that talent. Play to their strengths. Even side effects like low levels of aggravation or occasional exacerbations of tension can be accepted if the job is done competently.

In addition to allowing individuals to use their strengths, Phillips laid out a five-step process for increasing the chance of success of a project that can be applied to a team setting:

1. Understand all the facets.
2. Consider a variety of solutions including the potential consequences of each solution.
3. Take action that is consistent with administrative and personal policy objectives.
4. Communicate effectively.
5. Implement. (1992, p. 96)

If these five steps are constantly followed, the group will be able to move forward and succeed, regardless of the specific task. These tasks or missions can be accomplished by setting goals and weaving the vision into the process. Therefore, to be decisive, it is important to not simply follow a string of individual orders but to set up a system in which there is a continuous, uninterrupted process for moving forward. As both Pam and Tony told us, this process for moving forward is only enhanced by diversity, equity, and inclusion.

When working in a group and communicating, John White's value of empathy can play a big role. John, the former University of Arkansas chancellor who was both a cohost and a guest on our podcasts, believes you should first start with knowing yourself (which we will cover in more detail in chapter 4). A key question here is: are you living what you truly value? No one can know what they truly value unless they reflect on what is important to them.

John discussed how reflecting on what is important is highlighted through disappointments. When disappointments occur, it's often easy to blame ourselves, which can turn into a negative spiral. John turns this spiral on its edge and creates a positive experience. He believes disappointments help us develop and that getting through disappointments allows us to identify with others who have been disappointed. In addition, getting through disappointments allows us to recognize the importance and benefits of the experiences and, most importantly, how we can build on the disappointments.

John believes getting through his disappointments as a student and a professional helped him develop his emotional intelligence (EI), which is the ability to recognize, understand, and manage your emotions and those of others.

Developing EI requires you to start with knowing yourself. The toughest person you'll have to lead is yourself. In the deep recesses and dark places of your mind, what do you truly value and what do you want to be? Are you living those values? After you recognize yourself, any difficult situation that involves your emotions and those of others stops being about you and starts being about others. Once you really know yourself, then you can relate well to others and effectively communicate in group settings.

There are several concepts in communication that are related to authentic leadership. For example, one of the five dimensions of authentic leadership is consistency, which is a key component of Phillips's (1992) five-step process that can increase the chance of success of a project. Another concept is "knowing yourself," which John ties to what an individual truly values. If leaders don't know their own strengths and weaknesses, their ability to work in a group will be seriously compromised.

Using Emotional Intelligence When Working in a Group

EI is such an important concept for working in groups that it's worth exploring in a bit more detail. In his foundational *Harvard Business Review* article on the topic, Daniel Goleman (2004) points out that technical skills such as accounting, engineering, and business planning, as well as analytical reasoning and other cognitive abilities, do not translate into strong leadership skills. Having those technical skills and cognitive abilities should be considered a threshold capacity for a leader: they are required, but they are an absolute minimum.

Leaders also need a high level of EI. In fact, Goleman believes EI is twice as important as technical skills for strong leaders. This is especially important in a group setting when viewed through the five EI skills:

1. Self-awareness.
2. Self-regulation.
3. Empathy.
4. Social skill.
5. Motivation. (2004)

Self-awareness is knowing your strengths and weaknesses, what drives your values, and how these two areas impact others. Self-regulation revolves around controlling and redirecting any disruptive impulses and moods. Empathy, through the lens of EI, is the understanding of other people's emotional makeup. The fourth EI component, social skill, is absolutely critical when working with other people in group settings. It involves building rapport with others to move them in the desired direction. The fifth skill, motivation, is also important in group settings but is focused on the individual. Motivation is relishing achievement for its own sake and not for any sort of external recognition.

The good news is that these five skills can be developed. While some are easier to master than others, depending on the individual, all of the skills can be learned. This process involves having a colleague or coach tell you when you fail in one or more of these areas, then replaying the incident to elicit a better response. In other words, always fail forward by learning from your failures. This allows you to monitor your reactions and gives you the opportunity to intentionally expose yourself to situations and get feedback.

It's also helpful to observe others and learn from their actions. To work toward these ends, you need a sincere desire to master the skills and a determination to put forth a concentrated effort.

Being inclusive, having strong communication skills, being able to listen, decisiveness, EI, and having the proper mind-set for working in a group increases the effectiveness of the group. In addition, the EI skill of self-awareness is one of the practical perspectives of authentic leadership. While the other four EI skills are not directly related to authentic leadership, there are certainly aspects of resilience and optimism (two authentic leadership influences) in motivation, and empathy is strongly correlated to compassion (an authentic leadership dimension).

Nine Dimensions of an Effective Team

The Illinois Leadership Center (2006b) developed nine dimensions of an effective team that are helpful when evaluating the effectiveness of a group. For each of these dimensions, a series of guidelines on how to execute each dimension was provided. Theses dimensions and guidelines are intended to increase the productivity of the group:

Goals: clearly understood, relevant, enforce positive interdependence, generate high level of commitment.

Communication: accurate and clear, two-way, basis of all group functioning and interaction.

Participation: distributed, responsibility of all members, equalization, full use of all resources.

Decisions: flexibility, balance of time and resources, incorporate size and seriousness, commitment of all members, consensus.

Influence: equal through group, based on not only expertise but also ability and access to information, coalitions beneficial.

Conflicts: encouraged, promote quality and creativity, enhance commitment to implementing decisions, and should not weaken cooperative interdependence.

Cohesion: high, members should like each other and continue as a group, high level of acceptance and trust, encourage safety and change.

Solutions: minimal energy, eliminate problems permanently, need to sense problems, procedures should be in place for inventing and implementing, procedures should be evaluated regularly for effectiveness.

Intentions: high interpersonal effectiveness, consequences should match intentions.

These nine dimensions highlight the fact that authentic leadership is a strong leadership style when working in groups. Each dimension has components of intrapersonal and interpersonal behavior and plays on the need to balance these two components. This concept of balance is reflected in the "balanced processioning" which is one of the theoretical perspectives of authentic leadership and is a critical component of making decisions.

Key Takeaways

- Working in groups has many benefits, including exposure to backgrounds, experiences, and strengths that differ from yours.
- When working in a group, it is important to orient your mind-set to be inclusive of all members and to be willing to serve others. This requires consistency and compassion day in and day out.
- Another key component of working with others is strong communication. Communication is not just talking; it is also listening. This requires a strong sense of self-awareness to respect your perspective while also honoring the perspectives of others, as both you and

the people you are working with have unique perspectives. It also requires a tremendous amount of empathy toward others and yourself, especially when dealing with disappointments.

- Self-awareness and empathy are two skills of EI, which also includes self-regulation, social skill, and motivation. These skills are necessary when working in a group, along with the foundational technical knowledge of the subject matter.
- There are many guidelines available for an effective team, including the Illinois Leadership Center's nine dimensions: goals, communication, participation, decisions, influence, conflicts, cohesion, solutions, and intentions.

Value	Podcast
Collaboration and teamwork	Chris McCoy
Inclusion	Pam McGinnis and Tony Vinciquerra
Communication	Sam Alley, Troy Alley, Mike Johnson, John Reap, and Charles Robinson
Empathy	Charles Robinson and John White

Table 3.2. Values Discussed in This Chapter

CHAPTER 4

Me, Myself, and I

> **Points to Ponder**
>
> - Do you want to be the best or lead the best?
> - What are the six principles that can help you gain respect?
> - Which values fall under the umbrella of professionalism?
> - What is the importance of authenticity and passion?
> - How can you live an authentic life?
> - How will you answer the hard questions about yourself?

The number of people you meet and interact with over the course of your life will vary based on a number of factors such as where you live, what you do professionally, and, of course, how long you live.

Conservative estimates suggest that you'll meet at least ten thousand people, but that number can skyrocket to around eighty thousand for many people. In our roles at a university, for instance, we meet new students every year and interact regularly with alumni, business leaders, parents of students, and other academics. If you live in a big city, you might interact with someone new almost daily. And if you have a career in something like coaching, sales, or hospitality, you could meet dozens of new people every week.

Some of these interactions lead to relationships that will last for decades, while others result in relationships that last for years or even just a few minutes. However, there is one person who will be with you every day, hour, minute, and second of your life: you.

While it is easy to look outward during your leadership journey, whether with your mentor, your mentee, in a group, or in an organization, it is equally important to look inward.

This ties directly to authentic leadership. Bill George, the former CEO of Medtronics, points out that authentic leaders constantly refer to their developmental qualities in ways that tie those qualities to the five dimensions of authentic leadership (George 2003). In other words, authentic leadership requires that you channel your qualities into these dimensions. These qualities are tied directly to who you want to be, and you have full control over which qualities you choose and how you develop and use them.

George demonstrated how this plays out by linking his own five dimensions of authentic leadership to developmental qualities. Note, these will be referred to as George's dimensions of authentic leadership (to distinguish from Northouse's dimensions of authentic leadership). The link between development qualities and George's five dimensions of authentic leadership are shown in Table 4.1:

Purpose → passion
Values → behavior
Heart → compassion
Relationships → connectedness
Self-discipline → consistency (George 2003)

Table 4.1. George's Dimensions of Authentic Leadership → Developmental Qualities

George reinforces our belief that values are critical in all facets of leadership. This is highlighted by the fact that all of the developmental qualities he associated with his dimensions of authentic leadership are in fact values: passion, behavior, compassion, connectedness, and consistency. These self-focused values are lived out by being authentic. In George's discussion, he explicitly states that "integrity is the one value that is required in every authentic leader" (p. 20). Therefore, as we begin our conversation on how to bring out values when working on and with yourself, we turn first to integrity.

Living Out Your Integrity

Recording more than twenty podcasts leads to a lot of hazy memories about the discussions. There is one quote, however, that stands out crystal clear in our memories, and it was shared during the very first podcast recording with John White, chancellor emeritus of the University of Arkansas. The three of us were talking with John when he calmly said, "I would rather be the leader of the best team than the best leader of a team."

That quote sums up many of John's values, including the top five he listed (empathy, faith, flexibility, integrity, and vision) and the other values he holds that are apparent based on his actions, such as humility and honesty.

John, who helped us launch the podcast that led to this book, believes that integrity is the foundation for most values and that this foundation is a big part of being honest with yourself.

Integrity is a fascinating value. According to *Webster's New World College Dictionary*, integrity is "the quality or state of being of sound moral principle; uprightness, honesty, and sincerity" (2004, p. 742). Peter Northouse, meanwhile, defines integrity as a quality of "people who adhere to a strong set of principles and take responsibility for their actions" (2018, p. 25). So when John—a former chancellor, dean, assistant director of the National Science Foundation, and a member of five corporate boards of directors— essentially says that he'd rather be in a room of people who are better than him than to be the best person in the room, it lends credence to the importance of integrity.

John pointed out that one of the most challenging things leaders must deal with when developing and maintaining their personal integrity is the ability to deal with criticism. All leaders face accusations, some of which are fair and some that are totally unfounded. John believes leaders should respond to some accusations but choose to not respond to others. For example, he believes that if an accusation appears in a newspaper, it should usually be ignored. If the accusation is made by an individual, the leader typically needs to set the record straight—but only if the accusation is a challenge to the leader's integrity.

In the end, however, John doesn't believe in a cookie-cutter approach to responding to accusations. Unless your integrity is being questioned, it's usually best to remember the old maxim that if you are explaining, you are going backward. Therefore, if you are sticking to your true north and adhering to your fundamental values (that is, behaving with integrity), you should have confidence in yourself moving forward.

Respecting Yourself, Respecting Others

Another value that came up multiple times during our discussions with leaders was respect. Although it is common to discuss the importance of respecting others, it is also important to respect yourself.

Kim LaScola Needy, currently the dean of the College of Engineering at the University of Arkansas, believes that respect is one of the most important values for success as a leader. Self-respect comes from being authentic, being who you are, and knowing what you value.

When you have developed a healthy, strong respect for yourself, you can lead authentically and earn the respect of others. People don't want to hear about what you've accomplished, Kim told us: they want to hear about how you will help them. Therefore, when you want to get people on board, you need to be authentic and earn their respect.

Because people are always watching, listening, and observing, you need to earn, nurture, and increase their respect for you. Respect can never be assumed, especially in new settings that are created by transitions. While your reputation might create expectations when you start a new role, transitions reset your external respect to zero. No matter where you are in your career or what you've done in the past, you need to earn a new group's respect.

Kim has more than twenty years of teaching experience, and she told us she still needs to earn students' respect at the beginning of each semester when she walks into a classroom. We all accumulate credentials during our careers, Kim said, but students don't automatically give you respect: you have to earn it. It doesn't matter how many awards you have won, how many papers you have published, or how many patents you have received.

Respect, Kim added, isn't just something you earn, it's something you give. To create mutual respect, for instance, she makes it a point to arrive for classes on time, be organized and prepared for each lecture, and constantly communicate effectively. Showing respect toward students sets the culture for the classroom, and Kim has found that respect is then returned to her from students.

Respect, like integrity, also has direct ties to authentic leadership. Kim tied the concept of respect to authenticity and self-awareness. If a person is authentic, they are very comfortable with themselves and they know themselves. It is not a surprise that "knowing themselves," and the extension of authenticity, is one of the practical perspectives of authentic leadership, as authentic leadership requires a person to know themselves. In addition, self-awareness—an aspect of knowing yourself—is one of the theoretical perspectives of authentic leadership. Thus, there are strong ties among respect, authenticity, self-awareness, and authentic leadership.

The concept of respect is woven throughout "The Work of Leadership," a 2001 *Harvard Business Review* article by Ronald Heifetz and Donald Laurie. The authors propose six principles that can help you gain the respect of a group or organization:

1. Get on the balcony—move back and forth between action and a wider perspective.
2. Identify adaptive challenge—serve people, act on trust, respect individuals, and promote teamwork across boundaries.
3. Regulate distress—balance between feeling the need for change and being overwhelmed by change.
4. Maintain discipline—address perspective collectively.
5. Get work back to the people—deepen debate with questions, sharpen sense of responsibility, and demonstrate need for collaboration.
6. Protect voices of leadership from below—people often look up the chain of command. (Heifetz and Laurie 2001, pp. 131–41)

These six principles all contain strong components of respect. Considering the concept of self-respect, it is important to have self-confidence to use self-respect in your daily activities. Heifetz and Laurie point out that people aren't born with self-confidence: instead, self-confidence comes from success, experience, and the environment. Confidence is one of the influences of authentic leadership, and achieving it requires not only self-respect but also a high level of respect for everyone you are working with. Key components of professionalism can help you achieve confidence.

An Admiral's Professionalism

One component of true north for Mike Johnson, the associate vice-chancellor for facilities at the University of Arkansas who retired in March 2021, is his value of professionalism, a value that is particularly important when considering how you lead yourself. There are many ways to define professionalism, Mike told us, but he sees it including varying degrees of communication, interaction, technology, and other facets of the business world.

As long-serving academic deans, for instance, we (Matt and John) can tell you the number one issue raised by industrial advisory boards is the need to improve the communication skills of college graduates. The boards are looking for graduates who communicate in a professional manner.

Mike knows a lot about professionalism. Before his seventeen-year-career at the University of Arkansas, where he oversaw construction campaigns totaling more than $1.9 billion, Mike spent thirty-four years in the U.S. Navy. He rose to the rank of rear admiral, which is why he's respectfully known on campus as "the admiral."

Mike came to a university for his second career because interacting with students brought him joy and kept him young at heart (although it frustrated him at the same time). Thus, he intentionally invested in students in ways that went beyond what you might expect from a facilities manager. One of the investments he made involved professionalism.

Every semester, for instance, Mike talked with eight to twelve journalism students who were involved in a semester-long project centered on current building projects on campus. The students were required to set up an appointment with the admiral, and he expected them to come early and arrive prepared. If they hadn't done their research on the topic they were to discuss, they likely wouldn't get all the answers they needed.

During his meetings with the students, Mike made sure they spoke up, engaged him in discussion, established eye contact, and paid attention to the meeting rather than their electronic devices such as phones and computers.

Like many other faculty and staff members on university campuses, Mike is aware that employers are looking for people who not only can write well, sell products, and be creative, but who also can address an audience of one or many and engage with other people in a professional manner.

In the military, Mike frequently spoke to groups, contractors, and clients, and he had to learn how to ensure that those conversations were productive.

This type of professionalism is something Mike worked on throughout his career. Like with every skill attached to our values, the learning never stops. In fact, Mike believes that if he doesn't learn something new

Dimensions	Practical perspectives	Theoretical perspectives	Influences
Passion✔	Desire to serve others✔	Psychological capacities	Confidence✔
Behavior✔	Know themselves✔	Moral reasoning	Hope
Connectedness✔	Lead from core values✔	Self-awareness✔	Optimism
Consistency✔		Moral perspective	Resilience
Compassion✔		Balanced processing✔	
		Sage advice	
		Relational transparency✔	

Table 4.2. Breaking Down Authentic Leadership → Tying to Yourself

✔ indicates a direct relationship to an opportunity of leadership.

every day, he hasn't worked hard enough that day. We all should use that mantra!

Learning, building professionalism, and dealing with other people throughout your life are cornerstones of understanding yourself and developing a strong leadership foundation. No two situations are identical. People, environments, and situations change, so there will always be ways you can improve your professionalism. Therefore, you must know your core values but also be able to quickly adapt those values to changing situations. This is a key part of being an authentic leader.

This balance can be achieved in many different ways, but one common thread is passion. As with any activity, passion greatly enhances the execution of whatever task and the achievement of whatever goal you set yourself.

Authenticity and Passion: Two Sides of the Same Coin

Shelley Simpson, an executive vice president with J. B. Hunt Transport Services, listed passion as one of her top values, and she has woven passion into her work ethic and the work culture of J. B. Hunt.

Her personal work ethic was highly influenced by her father. Her first job at J. B. Hunt was an hourly role, but she worked hard because her father told her to take all jobs seriously. On her first day, Shelley had the mind-set that this was the last job she'd ever have. She also adopted the perspective that everyone you are working with is your potential future customer. This combination allowed her to excel in her role and to move up in the ranks to her current position.

Her passion for her work has remained strong regardless of her role. In fact, when we (Matt and Andrew) sat down to talk with Shelley, she mentioned that J. B. Hunt was hosting its annual Thanksgiving meal that day and that she and the other executives would be there to greet everyone.

Those brief conversations with employees, Shelley said, constantly reminded her about how hard they work and how deeply they care about the company. She fully recognizes that it is the frontline employees who make the company go. In fact, the next time you are driving along the interstate, take note of the trucks that are driving along with you. It shouldn't be long before you see a J. B. Hunt truck, regardless of where you are. Shelley made it a point to highlight the importance of the drivers of those trucks.

She spent time discussing how holidays are always hard for people, whether they are truckers away from their family or people reminded by the holiday of a lost friend or relative. Shelley believes small touches, such as greeting each employee on the way to the Thanksgiving dinner, can create a moment of connection between executives and front-line employees. By creating such moments throughout the year, long-term attitudes can be changed. These intentional reflections show the passion Shelley has for her role.

It is telling that Shelley discussed Thanksgiving and the fact that executives greeted all the employees on the way to the meal, as this is a demonstration of serving. Shelley admires servant leadership, and she is always ready to roll up her sleeves and support the front-line workers. Serving is one of the practical perspectives of authentic leadership, and it is a direct result of cultivating your passions.

Being Yourself, Being Authentic

Donnie Smith, the former CEO of Tyson Foods, is another leader who believes in the importance of authenticity. When we recorded the podcast episode with Donnie, he looked as if he was having a conversation in a friend's backyard. You wouldn't have thought he was the former CEO of the second largest processor and marketer of chicken, beef, and pork in the world.

Donnie thinks it is important to remain true to yourself and be who you are (that is, to stay true to your purpose, values, and principles).

When you have tough decisions to make, Donnie told us, you should fall back on your values—because if you don't violate your values, you will stay true to yourself. If people ask you to compromise, he said, it should be a pretty easy to answer "no" because authenticity is foundational.

This mind-set is especially important in job interviews, because the worst thing you can do is try to be someone you are not. If you are not authentic and you get the job, you set yourself up for struggles with the company because it has hired someone it was not expecting.

Donnie intentionally brought his authentic self to work each day and shared who he was with others by interacting with them on a regular basis. In fact, he learned early during his tenure as CEO that the people around him had come to expect him to behave in certain ways and noticed when he didn't.

One day after a particularly hard meeting, Donnie said he walked back to his office without really focusing on his surroundings. He hadn't been in his chair for more than five minutes when a colleague walked in and asked, "What is wrong with you?" Two employees had just asked the colleague if the company was being sold. Donnie had passed them in the hall without saying a word, which was highly unusual, so they assumed something significant (like selling the company) was going on.

Donnie's authentic self showed up when he was a leader who was engaged. A deviation from that behavior was cause for concern by his colleagues, and his silence had nearly scared the two employees to death.

Donnie said he didn't think anything about his silence, but the colleague said, "You don't get to not think anything about it." Donnie realized that regardless of what was going on, his team needed to see him living out his value of service. He owed the company a smile, and it went against his values to ignore people—even if he was distracted by weighty decisions. Donnie said he never forgot that during the seven years he served as CEO.

Being authentic in and around your team is a powerful way to improve your commitment to your values and to live them out in ways that energize others. For instance, the concepts of authenticity and the tie between your internal and external emotions were fundamental concepts for Abraham Lincoln.

In *Lincoln on Leadership*, Donald Phillips describes how the president spent as much as 75 percent of his time meeting with people—or, as he put it, "circulating among the troops" (1992, p. 13). In fact, Lincoln thought it was so important to be with people that he would often join meetings unannounced, making it a point to be accessible and amiable. Accessibility and amiability were key values to Lincoln.

Lincoln found that being among people gave him the ability to make quick and timely decisions (sometimes without relying on the word of other people), provide direction and leadership, and obtain accurate knowledge of others people's makeup and ability. All of these benefits increased people's awareness of Lincoln's compassionate and caring nature, a key to his authentic self.

For many leaders, however, living out these concepts during the global pandemic that began in 2020 presented a challenge unlike anything we'd ever experienced. The realities of COVID-19 caused practically all meetings to be virtual. The days of heart-to-heart and face-to-face discussions were gone. And while some people were forecasting the end of the office, we can tell you that all of us longed for the days when we once again could "circulate among the troops."

While there are still obvious unknowns about the future of work, companies are realizing that the amount of work-related travel could be significantly reduced, thus signaling a higher reliance on virtual meetings. This shift will require many people to adjust their personal attitudes and perspectives.

Regardless of whether we are meeting in person or virtually, however, some values will not and should not change. For example, Jessica Hendrix, president and CEO of Saatchi & Saatchi X, spent time talking about the importance of revealing your weaknesses and mistakes to those around you, and that type of vulnerability is valuable regardless of when or how you are interacting with others.

If you are pretending to be perfect, she said, you are only fooling yourself. Other people won't easily relate to you, and you certainly won't relate to them. On the other hand, Jess said, being transparent about your weaknesses and mistakes can earn trust, because people will know you are willing to tell the truth even when it's hard. You want people to feel comfortable.

We all make mistakes, but we want to acknowledge those mistakes and keep improving.

When you are having a discussion with Jess, it is easy to see that she is an authentic leader. We discovered this at the very beginning of our podcast interview with her, when we asked what she preferred to be called.

"I'm just Jess," she said.

She may have a title (president and CEO), but her desire is to effectively lead an organization of creative problem solvers who help clients succeed. She considers this the definition of success and of winning. Her official titles feel unnecessary sometimes, she said. At the end of the day, she takes responsibility, but she got those titles through hard work and a strong focus on the job at hand. And if she is not authentic, she would be able to keep up the continuous work and focus for only a short period of time.

Kim had a very similar perspective. She believes you need to admit mistakes and commit to improving so that you don't make the same mistakes multiple times. "I'm sorry" and "I made a mistake" are two powerful phrases that move relationships forward, she said.

This type of relational transparency is one of the theoretical perspectives of authentic leadership. For someone to apologize and own their mistakes, however, they must have confidence in themselves and what they believe in. This is a lifelong, iterative process that requires constant self-reflection.

Angela Grayson, the founder of Precipice, also talked about the importance of looking at yourself and working hard to maintain your values. One of her top values, as you might recall, was being ethical, and she pointed out that this is an area where leaders are regularly challenged by business opportunities, clients, and suppliers. You can't read the newspaper without learning about someone who has been involved in a scandal for not disclosing information (during an initial public offering, for instance) or for distorting numbers to make a deal.

Angela told us she had made a conscious decision to run her business with integrity even if it meant less wealth in the long run. In our opinion, however, being ethical actually increases wealth. For example, in my first full-time job as an engineer, I (John) had a boss who demanded that I falsify records to show high performance. After wrestling the decision and deciding not to do this, I got in trouble and was forced to take a lower-level job. Two years later, my wife and I returned to academe, where I have had the infinite satisfaction of knowing I have spent my life using my God-given gifts. I am not wealthy by some standards, but I am a billionaire when it comes to life satisfaction. That satisfaction started with making an ethical, yet painful, decision.

As you move through your career, it is important to keep an eye on yourself, especially as more and more challenges are put on your plate. This calls into importance the concept of balance, which is another value that Jess listed. The plate doesn't get bigger, she said, and time doesn't increase, so you need to be smart about how you fill that plate.

Jess sees balance as a stool with three legs: professional vocation, family, and self. She recharges her batteries by paying attention to the third leg, herself, and that includes time for her spirituality, fitness, and solitude. Jess's role at work requires extensive travel, going to many dinners, and spending a lot of time in public settings, so she deliberately finds time to be alone. Working out at home or at the gym, she said, gives her time for meditation and solitude, which are key parts of her balance.

When she is not feeling great about being a good leader, mom, or wife, she said, it is probably because one of the legs is out of balance. She can function in an unbalanced state for short periods of time, but she needs balance in the long term to feel good.

It should come as no surprise that authentic leadership again finds a place here. The concept of balance-processing, which is a part of the concept of balance, appears in authentic leadership as one of the theoretical perspectives. Therefore, as we've seen again and again, authentic leadership and values-based leadership go hand in hand.

Answering the Hard Questions

You've now read several stories and perspectives on how others have built a strong personal foundation that enables them to achieve professional success. It is easy to read about other people, but much harder to implement these ideas yourself. There are several questions you can ask to begin or continue your personal development journey.

President Theodore Roosevelt is known for many things, including this quote: "nothing in this world is worth having or worth doing unless it means effort, pain, difficulty" (1910). This is often condensed into the more familiar phrase, "if it isn't difficult, it isn't worth doing." Keep this phrase in mind when answering the following questions, which come from the famed management expert Peter Drucker (1999). They will force you to look at who you are, how people see you, and how you want to be seen.

- What are your strengths? (Compare the long-term outcomes you achieved with the results you anticipated. When the actual outcomes match your anticipated outcomes, these are your strengths.)
- How do you work? (Consider how you communicate and obtain information. Are you a listener, a questioner, a reader, a discusser, or a combination of these styles?)
- What are your values? (Identify and list your core values. If you lead from your core values, which is one of the practical perspectives of authentic leadership, you will never go wrong. By reflecting on your core values, you can fall back on these values when you find yourself in a tough spot.)
- Where do you belong? (Reflect on the environment for situations where you thrive. How can you recreate these environments, and what resources do you need around you to create and maintain these environments?)
- What can you contribute? (Use your strengths, work ethic, values, and preferred environment to maximize your contribution to your organization.)

Like anything else worth asking, these questions won't always have easy answers. By constantly addressing them, however, you can continue to feel comfortable with who you are. At the end of the day, you are the only person you will be with your entire life, so it is important to know who you are and what you need to reach your potential.

Key Takeaways

- Critical values to consider when thinking about yourself include integrity and professionalism, which will help you identify and follow your true north.
- The concept of true north is not static: your true north may change based on things you learn today or tomorrow. This requires you to have an open mind and a willingness to improve yourself, mind-sets that require discipline and respect, day in and day out.

- Regardless of where you are in your career, you will always meet people that you do not know, which means you are starting from square one in developing relationships and establishing your character. People are always watching, listening, and observing, so gaining respect from others is something that you need to focus on every day, and each new encounter begins with what is inside you.
- From getting on the balcony to maintaining discipline and identifying adaptive challenges, there are numerous ways to find strength in your core values and to channel authentic leadership.
- The easiest way to do this is to know yourself and then be authentic. Find your passions and run with them. Own your strengths and weaknesses. This will allow you not only to improve your weaknesses but also to leverage your strengths—which in turn will help you when you are being mentored, in a group, going through a transition, or mentoring someone. Perhaps most important, however, it will help you with yourself, the only person with whom you will spend every minute of your life.

Value	Podcast
Integrity	Sam Alley, Troy Alley, Mike Duke, Mike Johnson, Kim LaScola Needy, Pam McGinnis, Mario Ramirez, Shelley Simpson, Donnie Smith, and John White
Professionalism	Mike Johnson
Communication	Sam Alley, Troy Alley, Mike Johnson, John Reap, and Charles Robinson
Respect	Kim LaScola Needy
Authenticity	Greg Brown, Jessica Hendrix, Kim LaScola Needy, and Shelley Simpson, Donnie Smith
Humility	Donnie Smith, Charles Robinson, Mario Ramirez, and John White
Ethical	Angela Grayson
Balance	Jessica Hendrix

Table 4.3. Values Discussed in This Chapter

CHAPTER 5

Navigating Uncharted Waters

Points to Ponder

- Why are trust, honesty, and integrity the best policies in any situation?
- What is the importance of failure when it comes to innovation?
- How can you open your mind to imagine new combinations of solutions for doing things?
- What is the difference between leading and managing?
- What are the seven suggested ways to deal with change?

S teve White and his family were living in Denver in 2020 when he retired as president of the West Division of Comcast Cable. He was eager to spend more time with his wife and son, while also devoting energy to corporate board work, writing and speaking, and playing a part-time role as an advisor to the Comcast CEO.

None of those things required him to stay in Denver, but White had no immediate plans to leave.

White had grown up in Indianapolis, gone to college at Indiana University, and then relocated fourteen times in a career that started in medical supply sales and included several other industries before he settled into the cable business. He knows where the locals eat in Chicago, New York, Atlanta, Los Angeles, Denver, and a number of other smaller cities. So while he's now happy to call Colorado home, he can tell you all about what it's like to go through transitions.

"Once we discover that the straight path to success is actually crooked," White points out, "we quickly encounter another reality: There's a ton of uncertainty on a crooked path" (White 2022).

White's career trek might seem crazy to you—or maybe you have U-Haul on speed dial, and White's journey sounds pretty normal. Regardless, when you think about it, life is a constant series of transitions for everyone. In fact, the median job tenure in the United States in January 2020 was only 4.1 years (Bureau of Labor Statistics 2020). Even if you stay with the same company in the same town for your entire adult life, you will likely assume new roles and work on different projects along the way. In addition, you'll have all sorts of transitions in your personal life, many of which will have an impact on who you are and how you lead.

Transitions can be especially challenging for leaders because they typically come with high levels of uncertainty and a process full of unknowns. Many of the tools and skills you developed to get you where you are will no longer work, so you have to adapt, pivot, and grow.

No matter where you go or what you do as a leader, however, your values need to go with you if you want to succeed as an authentic leader. In fact, it's your values that will lead you into transitions, help you navigate them, and successfully take you out of them.

An Anchor in the Storm

Integrity, the most common value listed during our podcast discussions, is a strong anchor in the storms of transitions.

Troy Alley, executive vice president and chief operating officer of Con-Real, told us that without integrity, you can't achieve anything of real value. Integrity is the building block for trust, and without trust nothing worthwhile can be accomplished in business or your personal life. When you tell someone you're going to do something and you do it, you'll see a three- or fourfold return on your investment—maybe not right away, but eventually. The return may be measured in perceptions rather than dollars, but it will be valuable nonetheless.

When Troy was raising his children, he often shared stories that taught them life lessons about values such as integrity. On the podcast, he told us one of these stories—about a contractor who was going through hard times. A friend asked the contractor to build him a house. The contractor agreed, and the friend said, "Don't worry about the cost, I'll take care of it."

The contractor, however, decided to skimp on materials and ended up building a $100,000 house for $70,000. From the outside, it looked fantastic, but the contractor knew it was full of flaws. What the contractor didn't know was that his friend already had two houses and didn't need another one. So when the project was completed, the friend gave the key back to the contractor, turning the house into a gift. Instead of making money, a lack of integrity came back to the contractor.

Troy's point is that you're always called to do your best work and be truthful. Regardless of the transitions you are experiencing, veering from that foundation will leave you with a house that might look nice from the outside but that won't last long because it's made of cheap materials.

In *Lincoln on Leadership*, Donald Phillips describes how trust, honesty, and integrity are the best policies in any situation. Abraham Lincoln would channel these three values by constantly acting on them, preaching them, and persuading others to follow them. This allowed Lincoln's followers to lift themselves out of their everyday selves. Phillips referred to Lincoln as a "sharing leader," which means a leader who helps others climb the ladder of success with patience, trust, and respect (1992, p. 54).

Lincoln valued trust, honesty, and integrity so much that he said he "stands with anyone who does right, and parts with anyone who does wrong" (Phillips 1992, p. 54). In other words, as we climb the ladder or help others climb it, moving closer to or farther from others based on their values will be a key part of transitions.

Integrity and authentic leadership converge during transitions when leaders consider how to apply values and morals. Several concepts of authentic leadership should be considered when these ideas overlap:

- People can learn to be authentic leaders.
- Authentic leaders try to do the right thing and work toward a common goal.
- Authentic leadership can have a positive impact in organizations.
- Critical life events shape and form authentic leadership by stimulating growth and greater authenticity. (Northouse 2018)

The last point is especially important when talking about transitions. While most critical life events are positive experiences, sometimes such events center on a failure or some other negative experience.

When people think of Walmart, for instance, they see the world's largest private employer and the largest company in terms of revenue. Dozens of transitions throughout its history, however, have worked together to shape the modern version of Walmart. And as we learned from Mike Duke, the company's CEO from 2009 to 2013, one of the most visible transitions turned into a significant innovation—even though it was born out of a failure.

Turning Failures into Innovation

Mike learned during his lengthy career in the retail industry that innovation can emerge from periods of transition or act as a catalyst for transitions.

Mike believes great merchants are great innovators because they constantly find ways to meet the changing needs of customers—providing new products, new services, and new ways to deliver those products and services. Whether innovations came as a response to or created transitions in the marketplace, Mike told us he enjoyed testing new ideas that had no predetermined solution to problems.

As a leader, Mike recognized that some new ideas would fail, but he also knew that a cycle of continued testing and retesting led to innovation and success. A key component of this mind-set is that a leader can't get rid of people every time they fail. Failure should be expected and accepted from coworkers as long as the people and organization are failing forward.

In the 1980s and 1990s, for example, Sam Walton, Walmart's founder, experimented with Hypermarts—stores that sold both groceries and general merchandise and were often bigger than 220,000 square feet. The format, based on a European model, included features such as a food court, an arcade, and a bank. The stores were profitable, but sales were well below projections, and expenses for things like heating and cooling the facilities were much higher than expected.

Instead of dismissing the idea of combining groceries and general merchandise, however, Walmart learned from the experience. The company shifted to the Supercenter concept, with smaller stores of around 125,000 square feet. Supercenters became Walmart's growth engine for many years. While retailers like Kmart and Sears stuck with general merchandise and struggled, Walmart now operates more than 3,500 Supercenters in the United States.

Walmart continued to experiment not only with formats, but also with just about every other aspect of its business—from using computer systems that revolutionized inventory management to delivering groceries or having them ready for customers to pick up. Walmart got where it is today because its leaders were willing to try different things, some that worked and some that did not.

Creating and surviving innovation transitions requires a mind-set that balances the need to manage standard tasks and the need to work outside of those tasks. Exactly how much to do, what to do, and when to do it is not always clear.

Mike remembered that during the early days of his career, he was able to do something that met the needs of the customer and immediately get positive feedback that fed his desire to help customers. This is an example of a balance that puts extra emphasis on the need to work outside of managing standard tasks. The greatest merchants are the greatest innovators: they identify the needs of customers and provide products to meet those needs, which yield services to benefit customers. Even according to supply chain theory, one should always be trying new things and testing new ideas. There is no solution that is predetermined for success. In fact, an idea that gets tested, usually fails but it is modified through more innovation, retested, and improved.

An excellent way to stimulate an innovation mind-set is by reading. In *The Contrarian's Guide to Leadership*, Steven Sample (2003) says that reading provides perspective and stimulates original thinking.

Sample divides influential texts, or what he calls supertexts, into three tiers and believes these texts contain critical keys to success. His first tier is the most influential and contains the Judeo-Christian Bible, the Qur'an, Bhagavad Gita, the Pali Canon of Buddhism, and the Analects of Confucius. It is interesting that these are the primary texts of the most prevalent religions around the world. These texts contain timeless truths about human leadership, human nature, and the potential of humans.

Sample readily acknowledges that readers must make their own decisions about what's valuable in these supertexts. The information from these supertexts, however, can provide insight into the possibilities during transitions. But whether you are reading supertexts or planning your next move, you need to be committed to moving forward and flexible with how to do so.

Dimensions	Practical perspectives	Theoretical perspectives	Influences
Passion	Desire to serve others✔	Psychological capacities	Confidence
Behavior	Know themselves	Moral reasoning ✔	Hope
Connectedness✔	Lead from core values✔	Self-awareness	Optimism✔
Consistency		Moral perspective✔	Resilience
Compassion		Balanced processing✔	
		Sage advice	
		Relational transparency	

Table 5.1. Breaking Down Authentic Leadership → Tying to Transitions

✔ indicates a direct relationship to an opportunity of leadership.

Staying Committed While Thinking Gray

Another value that goes hand in hand with transitions is commitment, which was one of Mike Johnson's top five values.

Mike, as you may recall, is the former associate vice-chancellor for facilities at the University of Arkansas and a thirty-four-year veteran of the U.S. Navy. The admiral, as he was known on campus, believes commitment is complex because it involves multiple parts that work together. His commitment has been to himself, his career, unit, wife, and kids. All of these things pulled at him as he made his way along his career path, and each element intertwined between his personal and professional life.

Early in his life, Mike made a commitment to educating himself, to his friends and colleagues, and to his values. This created a web of commitments. When he was in the Navy, he was committed to his military unit, the people around him, and the U.S. Constitution. He is also committed to his wife, Terry (they celebrated forty years of marriage while we were writing this book).

He is committed to his kids, but he also recognizes that he fell a little short in this regard during his younger years due to the time demands on him in the military. He and Terry decided she would stay at home—a professional calling in its own right—to help provide stability for the kids and aid in their all-around development into adulthood. He was gone a lot, and if he had to do it again, he said, he would have made sure to spend more time with their children.

In his second career, Mike developed a deep commitment to the University of Arkansas and its civil engineering department, even though he wasn't a graduate of the department or the university.

One way Mike strengthened his commitments through the personal and professional transitions of life was by purposely spending time reflecting on what he could have done differently. Sharing his retrospection has served as an inspiration to us all. He acknowledges that everyone makes mistakes, and we only go through life once. He finds balance by being simultaneously committed to continuous learning, his family, and his country. The concept of balance is a subset of balanced processing, which is one of the theoretical perspectives of authentic leadership.

Mike's commitment to continuous learning, family, and country requires a high level of what Sample calls "thinking gray" (2003, p. 7). Thinking gray does not mean people should be skeptical. Instead, it involves letting your brain imagine new combinations to solve problems. This includes different organizational priority combinations, as well as seeing how these alternative combinations will play out.

Since there is no such thing as an unbiased article or objective sound bite, it is important to interact with multiple groups and sources before making a decision. This is key because transitions involve many decisions and often occur in unfamiliar terrain.

There are some dangers to thinking gray, however, because it can lead you to form an opinion before all the facts are known or might result in the perception that you are flip-flopping on decisions. Regardless, the concept of thinking gray is strongly related to determining how to organize your commitments. Thinking gray also becomes important when transitioning your mind-set from management to leadership.

All Leaders Manage, But Not All Managers Lead

Chris McCoy, the University of Arkansas's former vice-chancellor for finance and administration, clearly saw the conundrum he presents when he says that leadership must be a value. This was amplified because, during our discussion, Chris made it clear that the five values he provided were what he considered "leadership values." If you are talking about leadership values, he asked rhetorically, how can leadership be one of those values?

To provide the answer, he spent a significant amount of time during our conversation discussing the differences between leadership and management: taking people to a better place where they haven't been before (leadership) versus keeping things where they are and making them run better (management).

John Kotter's "What Leaders Really Do" (1990) provides a phenomenal case study of this dichotomy. Leadership deals with creating change. Management deals with uncertainty and complexity. Leadership deals with setting the direction, aligning people to a vision, and providing motivation. Management deals with planning, budgeting, organizing, staffing, control, and problem solving.

Chris bases his understanding of leadership on values, and his values begin with serving people—an outcome of the practical perspective "desire to serve others" of authentic leadership. This fits under his larger leadership umbrella, which includes the leadership-management dichotomy. He serves people by taking them to a better place where they haven't been before (leading), versus keeping things stagnant and where they are. He felt that he could refer instead to vision, forward thinking, or other similar concepts, but he decided that leadership covers it all.

Humble Transitions

President Ronald Reagan had a plaque on his desk in the Oval Office that read, "There is no limit to what a man can do or where he can go if he does not mind who gets the credit" (https://www.reaganfoundation .org/ronald-reagan/the-presidency/reagan-the-man/ 2021). A slightly altered version of the quote is often attributed to another president, Harry Truman, but the saying dates back at least to 1863, when a Jesuit priest named Father Strickland said, "A man may do an immense deal of good if he does not care who gets the credit for it" (quoteinvestigator.com 2021).

The saying has been popular through the years among leaders who value humility, which is why a similar plaque sat on the desks of both

Donnie Smith (the CEO of Tyson Foods) and his mentor, Buddy Ray, who worked for Tyson Foods for fifty years. And when we interviewed Donnie, he drove home the point that this particular value is important not only when leaders are leading but also when they are transitioning out of leadership.

More than 120,000 people worked for Donnie when he was Tyson's CEO, but he saw himself as just another member of the team. It wasn't that he thought his work was unimportant. He just saw his work as his role, and that role was one of many that had to be filled for the company to succeed.

Donnie said it's easy for leaders to get wrapped up in self-importance, but he learned early on that leaders don't define a company. And never was that clearer, he said, than on January 4, 2017, when his retirement took effect. Donnie didn't show up for work that day, yet—as he pointed out—Tyson continued to operate just as it had the day before. If none of the people who worked in the plants had shown up, nothing would have been produced. If no one on the sales team had shown up, nothing would have been sold.

Everyone has a role, he said, but no individual is indispensable.

Empirical evidence suggests that the CEOs of major publicly traded companies make a difference and that the percentage of the market capitalization that they affect is high. But that's no license for arrogance, and Donnie always demonstrated humility in his leadership. We saw it firsthand, for instance, when he was Tyson's vice president of transportation and served on the advisory board for the Supply Chain Management Research Center at the University of Arkansas. Later, when Donnie was CEO, Tyson's stock price went up dramatically and the value of the company soared, but you never would have known he was at the helm of Tyson if you just met him on the street. Not only did he value humility, but he lived it, and that allowed him and his teams to successfully navigate each transition in his career journey.

Staying Flexible

Flexibility is the final value that our podcast guests viewed through the lens of transition.

John White, chancellor emeritus of the University of Arkansas, told us that learning from disappointments helped teach him the flexibility he needed during transitions. When he was younger, John said he was stubborn. It was the "White way or the highway," he said, or the "White way or the wrong way." It took time for him to realize that this attitude was not a path to success. Instead, he needed to change interactions by listening, being flexible, and realizing that he did not have all the answers.

John believes the answer is always in the room, but leaders need to be flexible enough to allow others to create it. Thus, he learned to go into a room with the mind-set of "I have a question" rather than of "I have an answer." Leaders need to remove "I," "me," and "my" from their vocabulary, he said, and replace those words with "we," "us," and "our." If you are striving to be the best leader of the team, he said, you will do what you think is right to achieve success because your mind-set is focused on yourself. But if you want to be the leader of the best team, then your focus is on the team. That requires flexibility.

Our interview with John was humbling. His career spans more than forty years, so it was enlightening to hear him say it takes a long time to be an effective leader. Rather than a destination, it is a lifetime journey that's full of transitions. That should bring optimism to us all, because it means that each of us can develop our leadership abilities.

Moving Forward with Change

While every transition has many variables, from the individuals involved to the starting and ending points, there are some steps that all leaders can consider when moving forward with change. One of the models I (Andrew) took from my time in the Illinois Leadership Center's I-Programs was the seven steps for dealing with change that were taught in the Ignite portion of the program:

1. Do not only look at processes, look at relationships.
2. Instead of controlling, shape; instead of predicting, find patterns.
3. Increase conversations within your team: up the chain, down the chain, and laterally.
4. Actively seek those with different perspectives.

5. Fill your toolbox: there is no one solution to every problem.
6. Stop, take a breath, breathe, and reflect.
7. Do not look for one right answer: explore multiple answers.
   (Illinois Leadership Center 2006a)

It is interesting that the first four steps all deal with the concept of connectedness (one of the five dimensions of authentic leadership). Whether we are connecting with people or trends, the concept is key. Therefore, by working through these seven steps when facing changes, you will have a higher chance of success with what you are leaving behind and what you are going into.

Key Takeaways

- While transitions often usher in new and exciting opportunities and challenges, they are also a cause of stress, with the high levels of uncertainty and multiple unknowns. During times of transition, it is important to stay true to your values and focus on authentic leadership.
- Regardless of your core values—trust, honesty, integrity, inclusion, communication, or anything else—sticking to them during transitions allows you to stay true to yourself, which will help you when you interact with others.
- Sometimes transitions are by choice, but sometimes they are externally imposed. Sometimes they come from successes, and sometimes they come from failures.
- While it is obviously more enjoyable to have a transition based on success, sometimes a transition based on failure can be more helpful. Failures often drive the need for innovation, from which new and better ideas and products can be born. And failures help us identify tools for improvement, such as books and workshops that provide a high return on the time and resources invested in them.
- Differentiate between managing a transition and leading it. Managing focuses more on the daily tasks that must be completed for a project or endeavor to be successful. Leading focuses more on setting the direction, aligning ideas, and motivating others.

- When you are comfortable and aware of your values, you are less likely to make decisions you may regret.
- When you can see connections, relationships, and patterns, you can come up with a suite of solutions that will provide the answers to whatever transition you are facing.

Value	Podcast
Integrity	Sam Alley, Troy Alley, Mike Duke, Mike Johnson, Kim LaScola Needy, Pam McGinnis, Mario Ramirez, Shelley Simpson, Donnie Smith, and John White
Innovation	Sam Alley, Scott Bennett, and Mike Duke
Commitment	Troy Alley and Mike Johnson
Leadership	Chris McCoy
Humility	Donnie Smith, Charles Robinson, Mario Ramirez, and John White
Flexibility	John White

Table 5.2. Values Discussed in This Chapter

CHAPTER 6

The Importance of Mentoring

Points to Ponder

- Why is being a mentor helpful if you want to build leaders?
- How does being a mentor improve your ability to set a direction and cast vision as a leader?
- What are the benefits of being a mentor?
- How do you pick someone to mentor?
- What are some best practices for mentoring?

As we mentioned in chapter 2, mentoring is an intentional relationship with a focus on supporting another person's long-term growth and development. Since the mentor generally has a larger and more diverse set of experiences, the mentee tends to receive the majority of the benefits in the relationship.

The mentor, however, also benefits from the relationship. Purposeful mentoring is highly beneficial to the mentor because it helps the mentor become a better leader, set direction, cast vision, relate to and motivate other people, and increase their sensemaking skills—the ability to constantly understand changes in the business environment and interpreting their ramifications for their industry and company. And from an organizational standpoint, being a mentor helps gain alignment throughout the organization and develop a culture that values mentoring.

Mentoring is essential to authentic leadership because it addresses personal and professional growth from the three perspectives of authentic leadership (as defined in Table 1.2)—intrapersonal, interpersonal, and developmental. Whether their relationship is informal or formal, mentors and protégés have the opportunity to look at their own values and beliefs about leadership, interact in relational ways that add value to both parties, and work together to develop their abilities over time.

By meeting regularly and with a specific focus, a mentor helps the protégé identify passions that lead to a strong sense of purpose; behave more consistently in alignment with established values; build bonds of trust by connecting authentically with others; and nurture greater empathy and compassion, which allow for more fruitful service to the needs of others. Passion, consistency, and compassion are dimensions of authentic leadership.

Mario Ramirez, president of MRamirez Group and an investment banker with Avalon Securities, has had a diverse career with various roles in multinational companies. When Mario was in college, he didn't know what his career arc would be or the twists and turns that it would take. We asked him what advice he would give his younger self, looking back on his career.

Without hesitating, Mario talked about being aware of and following your passion. He stated the importance of being true to yourself and others. While his first job after college was with Merrill Lynch, he wanted to move away from the brokerage business. He had many tempting offers from other brokerage companies, and he was running out of savings, but he didn't want to settle for a good job he knew he didn't really want. Instead, he went back to mowing lawns to pay the bills while continuing his search.

His commitment to passion led to a twenty-one-year career with TIAA Financial Services as a financial consultant. He went from working as an individual consultant, to a personal investment and trust consultant, the southwest director of wealth management, the national director of wealth management executive planning, and the managing director of executive relations and Hispanic markets. Even the last position was just a stepping-stone to pursuing his strongest passion, which was starting his own business. He launched MRamirez Group in 2017.

This type of intentional reflection increases your ability to mentor people in younger generations. You may not have been in your mentee's exact shoes, but chances are you've had many similar experiences with your job, friends, and family. Not only will you be able to help your mentee, but you will also help yourself.

The Benefits of Being a Mentor

While protégés develop immensely in their quest to become more trusted and authentic leaders, mentors and the organizations they lead also gain in many ways from mentoring relationships. Those benefits are often over-looked at first glance. Whether you are already a mentor or you are preparing to embrace opportunities to mentor others, here are some benefits to keep in mind.

Being a mentor builds better leaders. All the leaders we interviewed told us directly or implied in different ways that they were interested in developing other leaders. Mentoring is one of the most effective methods for doing that.

There's a huge need in the world for more authentic leaders, and thus leaders have a huge responsibility to mentor the next generation. In particular, there's a need to mentor the sorts of leaders who have great potential but who historically have been overlooked or undervalued. In other words, we need to make a more intentional effort to mentor diverse types of leaders—not just those with whom we have the most in common.

This is good not just for those leaders, but for everyone.

A scarcity mentality tells us that if someone else gets more, we get less. But an abundance mentality tells us that making any individual better off will make the entire organization better. Sam Walton, Walmart's founder, had a rule about respecting the individual, which plays to an abundance mentality because it tells us that by showing each person respect—and investing in that person accordingly—we all benefit because we expand the pie of capable leaders.

Mike Duke, Walmart's former CEO, pointed out that Walton never made categories that singled out which groups leaders should respect and develop and which groups they should not. Walton's basic belief was to respect every individual, regardless any factor—including gender, back-ground, ethnicity, or race. This meant every associate at Walmart should be invested in and developed by their leaders. If leaders ignore women, for instance, they are ignoring roughly 50 percent of their employees, which is bad for business and weak leadership.

John Reap, the former president and CEO of Town North Bank, pointed out that a willingness to help everyone grow as a leader actually starts by developing yourself. All leaders have faults and weaknesses, but the best leaders address their shortcomings rather than ignoring them. Developing yourself is a learning process. People are not born with leadership skills, but they can develop and learn those skills through making a concerted effort. Mentoring is part of that process.

Being a mentor develops a culture that values mentoring. An organization's culture is the set of beliefs that its people have in common. As people in your organization see you mentoring others (and being mentored), they will realize that mentoring is important to you. Many of them will begin to mentor others on their own. And if you create a mentoring process so that everyone is being mentored and mentoring and you participate in the process yourself, people will be more likely to buy into it.

Being a mentor improves your ability to mentor. The first time you mentor someone, it might be awkward. It will be easier if you have been mentored by several people over the years, but there will still be a learning curve that you can navigate only by experience. It gets easier as you adapt your strengths and style to the needs of your protégé and the situation.

There is no one-size-fits-all solution when it comes to mentoring. You may mentor someone in the office next door, or someone who lives and works in another city. One thing we all learned during the 2020 pandemic was that we can connect with others remotely for all sorts of purposes, and mentoring certainly is one such purpose. Each mentoring relationship helps you creatively develop a tailored approach for each new and unique mentoring relationship.

Some people are easier to mentor than others. For instance, you can dig into details more quickly with people who are more open, trusting, and honest because you don't have to spend as much time building transparency and trust into the relationship. People who are conscientious are easier to mentor because they will be better prepared when they meet with you. People who are agreeable may seem easier to mentor, but they may actually be more difficult because it can be harder to discover their real feelings and opinions. People who are moody can be difficult to mentor because they may periodically not want to participate, or they may be fearful about opening up.

The more people you mentor and the longer you are involved in mentoring, the more effective you will be in dealing with different situations and different personalities.

Being a mentor improves your ability to be mentored. Mentoring others helps you notice things that your protégés say or do that either facilitate or impede the process. This helps you respond more productively to your mentor. It's also another reason to encourage those you are mentoring to mentor others. When they are mentoring someone, they gain insights into the process and will respond better to your mentoring.

Being a mentor improves your ability to set direction and cast vision. When you mentor people within your organization, the richness of the information you provide about organizational direction is much greater than the richness you can provide through quick conversations, emails, and other lines of communication.

As you describe the organization's direction to your protégés, you will become more effective at explaining it. And because of the depth of the relationship developed in mentoring, you will have opportunities to modify and clarify that direction based on questions and suggestions from your protégés.

As John White, chancellor emeritus of the University of Arkansas, told us during our discussion, "To be an effective leader is not a destination, but a lifetime journey." Staying true to who you are and how you want to move through your journey requires a strong vision, he said. Mentoring helps you define and share that vision.

Charles Robinson, who was the University of Arkansas's Vice-chancellor for the Division of Student Affairs when we interviewed him and now serves as interim chancellor, also believes in the importance of vision. He believes leaders must look at an organization in a broad way and think of the particular challenges it faces. Then leaders must create an environment where new ideas can be born.

Charles created a strong vision for addressing the challenges associated with students from underrepresented groups at the University of Arkansas, and that vision resulted in a mentoring environment for those students.

The university requires that students must have a minimum score of 20 on the ACT to be admitted, but the average score for Black students in the state is 16. Charles believes that success on the ACT is based on what students are taught in their K–12 education and their familiarity with taking standardized tests. In the lower-income regions of Arkansas, school districts struggle to do well in these two areas.

To address these disadvantages, Charles had the vision to create a college access initiative. The idea was to go around the state to help high school students prepare for the ACT. In some ways, this can be seen as an institutional mentoring process, but it was Charles's vision and drive that got the initiative implemented. In that sense, he has become a mentor to each one of those students.

By creating this vision and obtaining the resources to achieve it, Charles showed an ability to mentor those working with him, as well as high school students he might never meet personally.

Being a mentor improves your ability to gain alignment. By mentoring people, you and your protégés tend to get onto the same page. As they mentor others, they also become more aligned with their protégés. If you have many people in the organization who are in mentoring relationships, the entire population of the organization will tend to be more aligned.

Being a mentor improves your ability to relate to and motivate others. Mentoring involves listening and understanding (being an "empathetic listener," as discussed above), both of which are core to being an authentic leader and which are two key components of developing strong relationships. By mentoring others, you learn to relate more deeply and accurately to your protégés and other people within their circles. The better you can relate to your protégés and their teams, the more strategic and intentional you can be in motivating them in appropriate and effective ways.

Kim LaScola Needy, currently the dean of the College of Engineering at the University of Arkansas, has built her ability to relate to and motivate others through her dedication to service. Service was one of the top five values that she listed. She believes that service and servant leadership are interchangeable. The desire to serve others is a practical perspective of authentic leadership. Her more tangible example of serving others is by getting involved in professional societies. As mentors, it is just as important to walk the walk as it is to talk the talk, and Kim does this by getting involved.

She advocates joining an association not simply for the sake of filling your résumé but for playing roles that benefit society. This builds up your network of professional contacts, and people notice when you are actively engaged versus passively attending. Kim demonstrates this commitment when working on committees at the University of Arkansas.

Dimensions	Practical perspectives	Theoretical perspectives	Influences
Passion✔	Desire to serve others✔	Psychological capacities	Confidence✔
Behavior	Know themselves✔	Moral reasoning✔	Hope
Connectedness	Lead from core values✔	Self-awareness✔	Optimism
Consistency✔		Moral perspective✔	Resilience
Compassion✔		Balanced processing	
		Sage advice	
		Relational transparency✔	

Table 6.1. Breaking Down Authentic Leadership → Tying to Being a Mentor

✔ indicates a direct relationship to an opportunity of leadership.

Being a mentor develops your sensemaking ability. The more you mentor, the more you develop an awareness of what's happening in and around your world. This awareness can be not only external: internal awareness can take the form of knowing yourself (a practical perspective of authentic leadership) or that of self-awareness (a theoretical perspective of authentic leadership).

Whether you are focusing on internal or external awareness, to make use of that awareness in mentoring, you have to make sense of how it relates to your protégés' situations. Over time, you develop a stronger ability to explain, often by asking the right questions, how trends and activities outside the mentoring relationship can affect your protégés' goals for growth.

Picking a Protégé

In *Greater Than Yourself*, Steve Farber (2009) describes a version of mentoring that goes beyond being helpful and is committed to seeing that the protégé eventually will be better at certain things than the mentor. If you are a master guitarist, for example, and you mentor an up-and-coming musician, the goal would be for that protégé to exceed your level of success as a guitarist.

Farber calls that type of mentorship an "act of love" (2009, p. 126). But while we can love everyone, we can't mentor everyone. In an article for Inc, Farber (2017) outlined seven criteria for picking the right protégé. We find Farber's list a great place to start when considering any mentorship, so here are our comments on his criteria (which he put in the form of questions rather than statements).

Pick someone you trust. You are investing ideas, insights, and information that are of value. In addition to advice and direction, you might share practical things like your contacts or personal things like your dreams and aspirations. Thus, you want to invest in someone who will respect and honor you and what you are sharing. It can be beneficial for the mentor and the protégé to have similarities in moral reasoning and moral perspective, as these are two of the theoretical perspectives of authentic leadership.

Pick someone you believe in. When you look at possible protégés, you will often see some candidates whose confidence falls well short of their potential. If you believe they can achieve far more than they realize they can accomplish based on their capabilities and character, then they likely would make good protégés. Confidence is important because it is one of the influences of authentic leadership.

Pick someone who could benefit from the help you can give. Just because you trust someone and believe in their potential doesn't mean you can help them. If you can't cook, you don't want to mentor a budding chef on the finer points of baking a chocolate soufflé. Think about your gifts and talents, especially as they relate to leadership and the particular challenges and opportunities potential protégés are facing. If they could benefit from what you know, become their mentor. If not, encourage and support them as a friend.

Pick someone who will use what you are giving them. This builds on the idea of trust. In this case, you want to trust that the protégé will have the passion, energy, and work ethic to take advantage of the mentoring relationship.

Pick someone whose values are aligned with yours. This applies whether you are picking a protégé or a mentor. In either case, it's important to be aligned on core beliefs, principles, and values. They don't have to be identical. As we stated above, there is great value in relationships with people with diverse backgrounds, experiences, and personalities. But leading from core values is a practical perspective of authentic leadership.

Pick someone you admire. A potential protégé should have something about them that you would like to see in yourself—such as character traits, a passion for a mission or cause, or an ability to motivate or inspire. If you don't admire something about a potential protégé, they might not be a good fit.

Pick someone you love. You might find *love* too strong or emotionally charged a word, but it really shouldn't be much of a stretch. At a baseline level, we would do well to love everyone around us as fellow human beings.

We bring energy and passion to the relationship when we mentor someone we care deeply about and when we are willing to serve and make sacrifices to see them grow and succeed. If we don't care for them in a deep way, we won't give the relationship what's required to make it fruitful. Even in informal mentoring, both parties will get more out of it if they care for each other.

Donnie Smith, the former CEO of Tyson Foods, talked openly about the value of loving and caring for the people in your organization. If you care deeply for someone, you will be open and honest about that person's vulnerabilities and weaknesses, which is a key ingredient of being a mentor.

For instance, supervisors should care deeply about their employees, but what happens when they fail to address weaknesses and watch as those weaknesses eventually yield major failures that hurt the organization? The question that then must be asked, according to Donnie, is, "Who failed to expose this weakness?" The answer is every supervisor who didn't address the relevant issues. Those supervisors might claim they cared deeply, but their actions don't reflect that claim.

One way to show love and care is to be a servant leader. Donnie was a serviceman early in his career, and he regularly talked to growers about how to raise chickens. He quickly learned that what he had been taught in college did not help him with most of what he needed to do. Therefore, he fell back on the concept of servant leadership and asked the growers, "How can I help you?"

He quickly realized that the growers needed an advocate to help them. If the growers needed coaching, he would coach. If the growers needed help fixing a brooder, he would help fix the brooder. While doing all of this, Donnie was known to tell his people that he loved them, but he also showed that love with his actions. How better to be a mentor than to ask the people around you, "How can I help?"

Some How-tos for Mentors

We mentioned above that there is no cookie-cutter formula for mentoring relationships. Mentorships involve people, and, well, you might have noticed that people are unique. Even very similar circumstances involving similar people will have nuanced differences that require fresh ideas and approaches.

For instance, let's say that you have led an advertising agency through a merger, and you had a mentor who helped you navigate those waters. Now, a friend is calling because her auto parts company has bought a competitor, and she must merge the two companies. She's asking you to mentor her, and you agree. But while much of what you learned from your experience will apply, some things obviously will be different.

There are, however, a few common best practices to keep in mind. Some of them you can discern from what we've discussed above about the benefits of mentoring and the things you should look for in a protégé. Here are a few more you can add to your list.

Define a project to work on. This applies primarily to formal mentoring relationships, although there can be exceptions. Often, the project is the impetus for forming the relationship, so it's pretty easy to define. At other times, you need to identify and define a project with the protégé. Early conversations might reveal that the protégé struggles to delegate and trust others to perform work, so you can then build a project around improving that ability. Having a project provides structure, goals, measures, and accountability, and the payoff is that it typically produces tangible results.

There are a wide range of potential projects to work on. For example, you could start with reading the *Harvard Business Review*'s "10 Must Reads on Leadership" (HBR, 2011) or you could find a leadership book to read together and discuss (just stop by any airport bookstore). You could set three short-term career goals (that take 3–6 months to achieve) and three long-term career goals (that take 1–2 years) and track the progress toward these goals over a series of meetings. If you are more ambitious, you could begin a podcast series and write a book based on what you learned from the people you interviewed. There are countless ways to move forward, but having the anchor of a project helps you stay on track over the series of meetings.

Be willing to get your hands dirty. Mentoring isn't always easy. It takes time and effort to prepare for meetings and follow up on commitments. Each of us has only twenty-four hours in a day, and we all have the same 1,440 minutes, or 86,400 seconds. Time is a finite resource, so taking the time to mentor someone will take time away from something else.

Before committing to a mentoring relationship, it is important to allocate the proper amount of time. A rule of thumb in academe is that every hour spent in the classroom requires a minimum of three hours of preparation outside the classroom. A similar time commitment is not unreasonable for a mentoring relationship.

In addition to time, you also need to be willing to open up to another person. Sometimes you must vulnerably share your weaknesses or faults to make points or earn a deeper level of trust. It is not easy to admit a weakness to yourself, and it is even harder to admit one to another person. While mentoring relationships should spend a lot of time building on the strengths of each individual, time should also be spent on identifying the weaknesses and building on those.

Mentor even when doing so is unofficial. Never pass up opportunities to help others grow, even if it's in informal ways. You might not see your role as a big deal, but years later you may learn that your fly-by acts of service made a huge difference in someone's career.

Many organizations have formal mentoring programs that partner specific employees. These can be excellent and should be more widely used, but don't feel constrained to have mentoring relationships only in programs like this. Keep an eye out for other opportunities, such as national-level committees, professional organizations, or even your local gym. Keep an open mind, and you may identify an opportunity that normally would have passed you by.

For instance, one of the ways that Kim LaScola Needy, currently the dean of the College of Engineering at the University of Arkansas, mentors others is by getting involved with professional societies. Her passion for serving others in this way is an example of a practical perspective of authentic leadership, and it allows her to lead by example in informal settings.

Although many formal mentoring programs have an official structure, an informal mentoring relationship is a blank slate. There are pros and cons to this, but in an informal mentoring relationship, you, as the mentor, need to be deliberate in thinking about how you can mentor, when you should mentor, and how you can communicate with the protégé in an effective manner.

Mentor by example. As a leader, you are under a microscope, and everyone you lead is looking through it to see what's there.

Pam McGinnis, president of global marketing at Phillips 66, became a supervisor at the age of nineteen and was advised to model hard work and integrity as a foundation for leadership. Doing the right thing—especially if it's hard, painful, and time-consuming—takes courage, she said, but it sets an example for others to follow.

As a new leader, she immediately leaned into some advice from her father: "Never ask anyone to do anything you wouldn't do yourself." This, along with working hard, is the foundation of integrity, which requires you to courageously do the right thing even if it is hard or hurts instead of being easy, fun, or fast.

Shelley Simpson, an executive vice president with J. B. Hunt Transport Services, recalled her early days with the company and how much she learned simply by spending time with leaders like Kirk Thompson and Terry Matthews as they worked together to reshape the company's pricing structure.

Shelley believes leading by example is a common value at J. B. Hunt. Whether in the private or public sector, people are always watching their leaders, she said. And they tend to stay with an organization when they connect in a positive way with the value system modeled by its leaders. If people are happy with their boss, they will not seek reasons to leave. While Shelley believes that there is no perfect journey to becoming an executive, following the concept of leading by example will never lead you astray.

Key Takeaways

- We all have something to learn, and we all have something to share. That principle is at the heart of mentoring relationships. As a protégé, you have something to learn from your mentor. But too many leaders delay mentoring someone else because they feel unqualified. Don't wait. Start today.

- Being a mentor builds better leaders; develops a culture that values mentoring; and improves your skills in being a mentor and your abilities to set direction and cast vision, gain alignment throughout the organization, relate to and motivate others, and develop your sensemaking abilities.

- When choosing a protégé, pick someone you trust, believe in, admire, and love; who will benefit from the help you can give and use what you are giving; and whose values are aligned with yours.

- There is no perfect framework for the mentoring process, but there are several best practices. Define a project to work on together, be willing to get your hands dirty, mentor even in unofficial ways, and mentor by example.

Value	Podcast
Integrity	Sam Alley, Troy Alley, Mike Duke, Mike Johnson, Kim LaScola Needy, Pam McGinnis, Mario Ramirez, Shelley Simpson, Donnie Smith, and John White
Develop people	Kelly Barnes, Scott Bennett, Mike Duke, J. R. Jones, John Reap, and Charles Robinson
Service	Jessica Hendrix, Mike Johnson, Chris McCoy, Kim LaScola Needy, and Donnie Smith
Lead by example	Charles Robinson and Shelley Simpson
Servant leadership	Scott Bennett and Mike Duke
Vision	Kelly Barnes, J. R. Jones, John Reap, Charles Robinson, and John White
Passion	Sam Alley, Mike Duke, Mario Ramirez, and Shelley Simpson

Table 6.2. Values Discussed in This Chapter

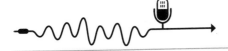

CHAPTER 7

Matching Company Values with Personal Values

Points to Ponder

- How well do your personal values align with your organization's values?
- What are the five biggest reasons why your personal values should match your organization's values?
- What is the relationship between values and strengths?
- Why should you exercise caution when considering values in the hiring process?
- How do you deal with friction between your personal and organizational values?

O f all the metaphors and illustrations you can find of an organizational structure for leadership, Donnie Smith, the former CEO of Tyson Foods, told us his favorite is the peach tree.

Most organizations are structured like a pyramid, with the CEO at the top, layers of management below that, and frontline workers at the base. Decisions start at the top and filter down. Unfortunately, employees in this model are often underresourced and overworked, while managers and leaders are often focused on metrics, stock value, and how they can climb to the top rather than on how they can support the people below them.

Some leaders suggest flipping the pyramid so that the CEO and other executives are on the bottom and the front-line associates and customers are on the top.

Bernie Marcus and Arthur Blank, cofounders of Home Depot, wrote about this in *Built from Scratch* (1999), and Frank Blake adopted the approach when he became the company's CEO.

Blake has pointed out that the inverted pyramid demands integrity from the leaders because they are at the bottom in a weight-bearing position. In addition, the important stuff happens above the leaders, so there's no room for pride; the forces of gravity work against them, so they have to push things up; and the focus is on supporting and serving others (Rakowich 2020).

The downside of this metaphor is that a pyramid resting on its point isn't very stable or safe, and its weight rests upon one or only a few people.

So whether it was top-down or bottom-up, Donnie found something lacking in the pyramid models. In his search for something that more accurately represented his values and approach to leadership, he came across Gordon MacKenzie's *Orbiting the Giant Hairball: A Corporate Fool's Guide to Surviving with Grace* (1998). MacKenzie's illustration of the peach tree helped Donnie seamlessly connect his personal values to the values of the organization he led, and he began applying the illustration, refining it, and teaching it to others.

When you think of an organization as a peach tree, Donnie told us, the leaders are the trunk and the workers are the peaches. What do peaches need to thrive? The basics are the nutrients that come from fresh air, sunshine, and water. If you walked up to a healthy peach tree, he said, and asked the peaches what they needed, they would say (assuming, of course, that they could talk) that they didn't need anything other than those nutrients (and time). They have all the resources they need to be great fruit.

How often would you hear a similar response if you asked the people you lead what they needed?

As part of the trunk, the CEO is tasked with supplying resources (people, money, and systems, providing stability with deep roots, and giving direction to the workforce. This enables the peaches to show up every day and do their thing with minimal instruction. They are given what they need to become great fruit.

The fruit, in Donnie's model, is the star of the show, and the leaders play a supporting role.

That illustration fits perfectly with Donnie's values, especially humility and service. And by applying the illustration, Donnie aligned his values with those of Tyson: "to be honorable and operate with integrity" (that's the stability of a strong tree trunk); "to be faith-friendly and inclusive" (that's taking care of all the fruit); "to serve as stewards of the resources entrusted to" it (that's making sure the fruit has the needed resources); and "to provide a safe work environment" (that's protecting the crop and keeping it healthy) (Tyson n.d.).

The Value of Matching Values

In some form or fashion, several leaders we spoke to for the podcast series echoed Donnie's idea that there is value in making sure your personal and organizational values match. Such matching is important to a leader for at least five reasons.

It affects the direction of the company. A key part of your responsibility as a leader is to set the direction for the company's future. Values provide a filter for analyses and decisions, which are involved in setting an organization's direction. If your values differ from or are at odds with the company's values, this will affect the discussions about the direction the organization should take, as well as the final decision on the direction.

It affects your authenticity. If your personal values are not aligned with the values of the organization you are leading, you may not be perceived as an authentic leader. Some leaders may feign agreement with corporate values in the short term, but, over time, the lack of alignment will cause the leader to seem inauthentic. The less enthusiastic you are about a corporate value, the more likely that feeling will be detected by other people in the organization. And if you are truly at odds with a corporate value, then that fact will almost certainly be noticed.

It affects your motivation. If your values don't align with those of the organization, work can become drudgery. The more strongly you oppose a value, the more that opposition will affect your desire to live out that value and execute your other duties. A lack of alignment also affects your ability to motivate others, because one of the ways leaders motivate people in their organization is through communicating the purpose of the organization. Values are a salient way in which purpose is communicated.

It affects how you relate to others. When organizational values are well established and clearly defined, a lot of information can be communicated with one word. For example, the stated values of the University of Arkansas's Sam M. Walton College of Business are excellence, professionalism, innovation, and collegiality, and they are summarized by the acronym EPIC. The college has specific definitions for each of these values, communicates those definitions and the importance of the values regularly in many different ways, and recognizes people formally and informally for living them out.

When someone does something that reflects those values, others will call the action "epic." And when someone refers to "epic behavior," everyone in the college knows exactly what it means. A leader in the college who doesn't value EPIC would be less likely to recognize EPIC behaviors and, therefore, less likely to call them out. The other leaders do so all the time, which affects how they relate to one another and would also affect how the leader with the mismatched values related to the faculty, staff, and students.

It affects your sensemaking skills. Sensemaking is an important leadership activity that involves explaining what is going on inside and outside of the organization in a way that reflects the values and direction of the organization. If you don't buy into some of the organization's values, then it's more difficult and less natural to make sense of the environment in a way that reflects those values. For instance, if you don't buy into a corporate value, you are less likely to think about the environment in ways that include the perspective of that value.

Tony Vinciquerra, the chairman and CEO of SPE, has seen the importance of matching personal values to corporate values in his leadership positions at CBS, Fox, and SPE.

When Tony joined SPE in 2017, he immediately recognized that the company needed to be reenergized around values. He told us that employees were applying standards that benefited them, not necessarily the company—which meant people were going in different directions. Tony tapped into his authenticity and made his core personal value of "always apply the highest standard" a corporate value.

To gain a better grasp of what was going on around him (using his sensemaking and relating skills), Tony interviewed employees at all levels of the company and discussed the opportunities and challenges they helped him identify. After these interviews, Tony fired nine presidents. These people had built cocoons around themselves, giving them a layer of protection but standing in the way of everything that needed to be done. While Tony's action was not what the nine leaders who were fired would have wanted, it made it easier for the other ten thousand employees to feel related to the company and motivated to do their jobs.

Dimensions	Practical perspectives	Theoretical perspectives	Influences
Passion	Desire to serve others✔	Psychological capacities	Confidence✔
Behavior✔	Know themselves✔	Moral reasoning	Hope
Connectedness✔	Lead from core values✔	Self-awareness✔	Optimism
Consistency		Moral perspective	Resilience✔
Compassion		Balanced processing	
		Sage advice	
		Relational transparency✔	

Table 7.1. Breaking Down Authentic Leadership → Tying to Organizational Values

✔ indicates a direct relationship to an opportunity of leadership.

Eliminating these nine silos provided air, space, and room for growth. With the bureaucracy trimmed, the ten thousand remaining employees felt a new urgency. Previously, weeks of what Tony called useless analysis were needed to move a project from being 95 percent finished to being 100 percent complete. Employees now adopted Tony's mind-set of getting 90 percent of the work done 100 percent of the time. This reduced the time-consuming and energy-draining tasks.

The decisions Tony made at SPE show the importance of direction, authenticity, motivation, relating, and sensemaking in leadership, as well as how applying his personal value of always applying the highest standards to the corporate world increased innovation and growth within the company.

When Values Aren't Strengths

Agreeing with your company values doesn't mean that those values will always be aligned with your strengths. There is a difference between strengths and values, and just like a person, an organization can have a value that is not a strength.

Values are what organizations and individuals aspire to put into practice, and decisions, strategies, and plans can help them make progress toward applying their values. Strengths can be defined in several different ways, but here we are talking broadly about your abilities.

Leaders who want to increase their self-awareness and emotional intelligence need to know their strengths and weaknesses. But it also helps to know which values need work and which ones are strong and can therefore be used to help the organization thrive. And it helps to identify opportunities for an organization to harmonize the strengths and weaknesses of each individual.

For instance, the "I" in the Walton College's EPIC values stands for innovation. This means the college wants to be innovative, to encourage innovation, and to turn out students who are innovative. This does not mean the college should not hire a leader who is weak on innovation: some positions are more operational and do not require as much innovation as others do. Therefore, a leader who is not innovative but who values innovation could use operational skills to facilitate the organization's advancement in innovation. At the same time, the college does need people who not only value innovation but also are innovative in their research, teaching, and leadership.

Although there are good reasons to consider values on both sides of the hiring process—those of the interviewee and the interviewer—caution needs to be used in any such consideration.

The first area of caution is related to diversity. If you focus too heavily on using values as a filter for selecting people for positions, you can wind up with too much homogeneity in your organization. You certainly don't want to hire people who are vehemently opposed to the organizational values, but you also don't want to eliminate candidates who would bring diverse perspectives, thus limiting innovation and new ideas that might be useful to the future of the organization.

John Reap, the former president and CEO of Town North Bank, discussed the importance of listening to divergent opinions, being open and inclusive, and being transparent in the process. Like many of our podcast guests, John found it hard to limit his list of personal values to just five, and the first things he talked about were his sixth and seventh values: know your weaknesses and hire to offset them (that is, harmonize your own strengths with the strengths of others), and be visible to your entire staff.

John strongly believes that a leader's purpose is not to bark orders. Leading requires not only communication, he told us, but also being physically present and visible to the team. When John was working his way up through the bank, he experienced both visible and invisible bosses, and he told himself that if he ever became a boss, he would be visible. When he became the CEO of two banks, he applied his personal value of being visible to the entire staff so that it became ingrained in the corporate culture.

A couple of times a week, he would walk around the bank. Whether he was talking to the top members of his leadership team or the janitors, he would simply be nice and use humor as a way to connect with people and learn information.

This was hardest while navigating rough waters, which is when many leaders (and their direct reports) want to hide in their offices. But interestingly, he said, this is the most important time to be visible. People know you are around and become more willing to talk to you, and through these conversations, you can address your weaknesses by tapping into others' strengths.

The second area of caution is related to alignment, because alignment of personal and corporate values is difficult to assess in an interview. Even looking at someone's history can be misleading in this regard.

While all leaders don't need to be strong in every value of their organization, they do need to aspire to live out each of the corporate values. One indicator of your aspiration to a value is that you yearn to pursue it: you desire to learn about the value, plan to improve in it, and are eager to invest your time and effort in it. In short, you are committed to making continual progress toward that value personally as well as continual progress in leading the organization to grow in that value.

Organizational values help you know which strengths to build on and which weaknesses to address. The values also likely identify opportunities to focus on mentoring or coaching. Some leadership coaches say you should focus on your strengths and build a team that covers your weaknesses. This idea seems reasonable when it comes to things like technical skills, but not when it comes to organizational values that are your weaknesses. Hiring people whose strengths fill the gaps where you are weak is wise, but it's not an excuse for staying weak. If you aspire to live out an organizational value that is a weakness of yours, then you will strive to make progress in addressing that weakness.

Also, when you invest time and effort in building a strength, then many times you grow in your appreciation of that strength and increase your resilience in that strength. If your weakness is an organizational value, working to overcome that weakness can help you acquire a taste for the value. And as you make progress toward overcoming a weakness that is an organizational value, you also gain insights into how to help the entire organization make progress in upholding that value.

In that way, aspiring to a value and building a personal strength or overcoming a personal weakness that happens to be a corporate value has a bidirectional effect. Aspiring to adopt a value turns that value into a strength, and building a strength that is a corporate value makes you aspire more to adopt that value.

Dealing with Friction

You can work to increase the alignment between your personal values and those of your company by creating a narrative about how well they align. Explain your values in your own words. If you do not know your values, then use online tools, articles, or a mentor to help you assess what you value. After you assess your values, write a short essay about them. Then read about the values of the organization and write an essay about them. Finally, write about the alignment between the two sets of values. This becomes your narrative on how your values align with those of the organization.

This exercise can help you identify important issues connected to your values. For example, most leaders will tell you that their organization values integrity. But this doesn't always mean integrity affects important strategic decisions. If you value integrity highly and you become convinced that your company does not, then you must work to change the organization's view of that value. Otherwise, it is time to start looking for another job.

When Donnie Smith was a young manager, for instance, he inherited a situation in which a group of people were doing something illegal. The behavior was widely known and had been going on for a long time, so

Donnie met resistance when he put a stop to it. He was even told he would be fired if he changed things. What was his response?

"I can find another job," he told us, "but I can't find another integrity."

That pattern persisted throughout his career. When he became CEO, Tyson's legal reserves dropped by 70 percent because everyone had realized his personal value of integrity was aligned with the organization's stated value of integrity. The reason to do the right thing, he said, was because it was the right thing.

Just like the misalignment in values early in his career, another example of where misalignments are often found is with servant leadership. If you are in a traditional, hierarchical organization, then it may appear that the organization doesn't value servant leadership. This is not to say that some of the leaders don't value it, but that on balance, such leadership is not really practiced throughout the organization. If the gap between how much you value servant leadership and how it's valued by the organization is wide, this can be a source of irritation, and it may be a good idea to look for a new job.

Giving back is another organizational value that can create friction when it's not aligned with your personal values. That is, if you highly value giving back and your company does not, then you may be more satisfied in an organization that continually prioritizes that value.

Sometimes the personal and organizational values might be the same, but a problem arises when it comes to how they are lived out. For instance, you and your organization might share the importance of family as a value. For you, that might mean you value getting home for dinner every night and spending quality time with your spouse and children. For the organization, it might mean employees' spending nonwork time together like a family.

John Roberts, president and CEO of J. B. Hunt Transport Services, told us three very powerful stories about how he put his family first at various points of his career.

The first story was about an incident that occurred in 1997, when John was relatively new to J. B. Hunt. He received a call while on vacation with his wife and two young kids. Several top leaders in the company's Dedicated Contract Services (DCS) division had resigned, and the CEO was giving John a field promotion.

At this point, DCS was only four years old and had approximately $150 million of revenue (in 2020, DCS had approximately $2.2 billion of revenue). The catch? A plane was on the way to him, so he needed to cut his vacation short.

Imagine yourself standing in a hotel room and hearing your boss ask you to sacrifice planned time away with your family so you could take over a cornerstone division of the company. What would you do? What would you say?

John's first thought was, "I need to talk to my wife."

Instead of thinking of career advancement, the increase in salary, and the movement up the ladder, John immediately went to his core value of family. He told his boss to wait and sat down with his wife to discuss the situation with her. Together they decided that he should take the job. John said he has never had a fight with his wife about work, because he always consults her about the big decisions that will immediately and directly impact their family life.

The second story was about something that happened later in his career, when he was fortunate enough to have a personal assistant. One day he was in a meeting when his wife called and couldn't get through to him. She was very upset, but she didn't know that John had a new assistant. And John had not made clear to his new assistant that he was never too busy to take a call from his wife.

Later, instead of just mentioning to the new assistant that calls from his wife should always take priority, John took the opportunity to challenge his entire team. He asked them if they attended their children's swimming lessons or dance recitals. He told them that he wanted them to put in eight solid hours of work each day, but then to be home for dinner and an evening with their families. In other words, he made it a point not only with his new assistant but also with others around him to say that prioritizing family is a good thing in practice, not just in theory.

The third story refers to something that John has done throughout his career. Many of us live off our calendars. We constantly strive to keep them current, so others can schedule meetings with us at times when there are no conflicts. John makes it a priority to place all the important family events on his work calendar. Whether it's a child's baseball game or recital, John treats his family's activities on an equal level to his business commitments.

That way he doesn't have business meetings scheduled that overlap with his family commitments.

John's view of family as a value matched J. B. Hunt's organizational view of it as John was working his way up as a leader. And as a leader, he made decisions and took actions that reinforced the alignment around that value.

It is interesting that another leader, Greg Brown, the chairman and CEO of Motorola Solutions, also places the utmost importance on family. John White interviewed Greg for our podcast, but I (Andrew) also happened to be present on a day in 2013 when John and Greg were discussing leadership. John asked Greg how many baseball games his son had had during Greg's career, and Greg immediately said "215." John then asked Greg how many of his son's baseball games Greg had attended in that period. Greg immediately said "214." While this topic did not come up during Greg's LeadershipWWEB podcast, we think it's safe to assume that the 99.5 percent attendance rate has not changed significantly over the years.

John Roberts and Greg Brown clearly show how leaders can successfully align their personal value of the importance of family with their corporate lives and corporate values without suffering long-term harm to their careers.

Rewarding Value Alignment

Shelley Simpson, an executive vice president with J. B. Hunt Transport, helped her company launch its Integrated Capacity Services (ICS) division, which helped the company become a major competitor in brokering as a third-party logistics business. This was a huge challenge for a company that traditionally had sold only its own trucking or intermodal services, so Shelley used her personal values and the company's values to create an alignment across her new team.

The three core values of ICS—accountability, commitment, and teamwork (ACT)—aligned with J. B. Hunt's values and Shelley's values. However, she needed to ensure that the ACT values became institutionalized within her team, which was a mix of internal hires who were well versed in the company's ways and outsiders who had more brokerage experience but were adapting to a new culture.

Shelley told us her senior leadership team spent a great deal of time coming up with the ACT values. More important, they spent a great deal of energy sharing what the values looked like in practice and rewarding the employees who demonstrated them in their work. The leadership team had ACT awards, including a monthly award for someone selected not by the team but by peers. And phrases like "now BTGT"—meaning "now, be the go-to person"—became commonplace within the organization.

To institutionalize those values, Shelley said she had not only to reward them, but also to live them. Work ethic, she told us, is the most underestimated value. People watch you from the time you enter management and especially when you hit the executive level, she said, and they stay with an organization because of the value system modeled by the leaders.

Creating bridges between your personal values and corporate values takes work, but that work is much more straightforward when the two sets of values are closely aligned. To create bridges between the two sets of values, it is important to have strong self-awareness and transparency related both to your values and to your understanding of the corporate values. This ensures a high level of confidence and resilience when you reflect on the intersection of your personal values and those of the company you work for.

Key Takeaways

- There are at least five reasons to make sure you have a match between your personal and organizational values:
    1. It affects the direction of the company.
    2. It affects your authenticity.
    3. It affects your motivation.
    4. It affects how you relate to others.
    5. It affects your sensemaking skills.
- Values are what organizations and individuals aspire to put into practice, while strengths are about your abilities. Like a person, an organization can have a value that is not a strength.
- Leaders need to know which values are strengths and which are not.
- If you focus too heavily on values as a filter in your hiring process, you can wind up with too much homogeneity in your organization.

- It is difficult to assess the alignment of personal and corporate values in an interview.
- Leaders don't need to be strong in every value of an organization they lead, but they do need to aspire to live out each of the values.
- Identifying your personal values and how they align with corporate values helps you identify and address gaps, or misalignments, that can be sources of frustration.
- Recognizing and rewarding others who live out important values is a powerful way to institutionalize those values.

Value	Podcast
Humility	Donnie Smith, Charles Robinson, Mario Ramirez, and John White
Service	Jessica Hendrix, Mike Johnson, Chris McCoy, Kim LaScola Needy, and Donnie Smith
Highest standard	Tony Vinciquerra
Integrity	Sam Alley, Troy Alley, Mike Duke, Mike Johnson, Kim LaScola Needy, Pam McGinnis, Mario Ramirez, Shelley Simpson, Donnie Smith, and John White
Family	Greg Brown and John Roberts
Work ethic	Greg Brown, Angela Grayson, Pam McGinnis, and Shelley Simpson

Table 7.2. Values Discussed in This Chapter

Leaders Inspire Us

Stu Todd, the founder and managing principal of Compass Partnership Marketing (CPM), sat down with two of us (John and Andrew) in a studio in northwest Arkansas on December 4, 2019, and we recorded a fantastic conversation about the importance of being genuine, not jumping to judgment, valuing merit, deflecting credit, accepting blame, and having fun.

The three of us were chatting as we walked out of the studio after the session, and Stu stopped in his tracks.

"I can't believe I forgot the banana!" he said.

We thought that maybe he had brought a snack to the studio and simply left it behind. We were wrong. Standing at the elevator, Stu shared one more story with us. Since it didn't make it into the podcast, we're thankful for the opportunity to share it here.

Stu founded CPM in 2008, but back in 1996 he was applying for a new job with a global company. He had made it through the first rounds of interviews with no problems and was flown to Florida for a final round of in-person interviews.

Stu checked in to an Embassy Suites hotel, and the next morning an executive from the company met him in the lobby for breakfast. Stu, who was not as concerned about his health as he is now, took full advantage of the hotel's fantastic buffet, which was included in the price of his room. The executive had a banana.

Stu and the executive talked throughout the breakfast, and on the way out, the executive stopped and indicated that he needed to pay his tab. He told the hostess he was not a hotel guest, and he paid $12 for his breakfast.

Twelve bucks. For a banana. From an executive whose company spent thousands of dollars a year on hotel rooms.

It was a classic example of integrity, and one Stu told us he will never forget.

Stories like that explain how we (Matt, John, and Andrew) know that values matter and why we believe in authentic leadership. Sharing stories like that is why we wrote this book.

This isn't an academic treatise on leadership theory, nor have we presented an exhaustive review of the literature connected to leadership. We simply conducted podcast interviews with twenty-three accomplished leaders we deeply respect and shared the highlights of what we learned about authentic leadership.

We lead mainly in academe, while most of the podcast guests were in industry—ranging from entrepreneurs to executives with Fortune 500 companies. We trust their perspectives holistically. We trust their values, whether personal, professional, or through a lens of leadership. And likely no one has learned more from the interviews we did with them than we have.

We focused on values and authentic leadership because all the interviewees are authentic leaders. We can affirm this because we know them personally and we've witnessed how they've led through the years.

It was no real surprise that ten of the twenty-three leaders listed integrity as one of their top five values, while nearly all the rest implied that integrity is important. What does this tell us? Authentic leaders ooze integrity. You see it in all aspects of their lives. This is why integrity was integrated into each chapter. We see it as the glue in authentic leadership.

Mentoring was another important theme that emerged in our discussions, which is why we devoted two chapters to the topic—one to the concept of having a mentor and another to being a mentor. Mentoring was not a common value among the interviewees, but it was a common best practice in their leadership development and can have a large impact on leaders' lives and careers.

In fact, mentoring is the secret to an organization living out its vision. Jim Coffman, a legendary provost and chief academic officer at Kansas State University, told me (John) that a vision is something an organization naturally aspires to become. And Jim Collins, the author of "Good to Great" (2001), points out that if an organization is trying to realize a single vision, bureaucracy and red tape are minimized. Why? We contend that successful organizations are full of what Malik Sadiq, chief operating officer at the LIVEKINDLY Collective, calls owners. Successful organizations are full of individuals who own what they do. How do you find owners? You develop them. How do you develop them? Mentoring. Simply put, this is the secret of high-performance organizations. Mentoring develops the owners who fuel the vision.

To be authentic, you must know yourself. All the leaders we interviewed know their strengths, challenges, and opportunities to improve. They depend mightily on mentors and mentees to gain self-awareness, learn from mistakes and difficulties, and act on their values.

Because they know themselves, they are humble. We will never forget the podcast with Donnie Smith, the former CEO of Tyson Foods—the world's second-largest meat processor. He sat in our office with his backpack on the floor and had an unmistakable common Joe presence.

And John White, who was interviewed for the podcast series and was a cohost for other episodes, often humbly weeps as he describes his experiences as chancellor at the University of Arkansas. Through his leadership, the university transformed itself from a land-grant university with a mostly regional presence to a nationally competitive institution. In particular, his leadership of the Campaign for the 21st Century resulted in more than $1 billion in gifts to the university. The authenticity of his desire to change his alma mater and state is as fresh as it was when he became chancellor in 1997.

Humility was a virtue we saw in the leaders we interviewed, but it wasn't always mentioned when we asked them to provide their top five values. That question yielded fifty-two unique values. Twenty-nine values were mentioned once, and ten were mentioned twice. While there could be some discussion as to whether one or two of these values could be combined, the sheer quantity of values was interesting. More interesting, however, were the values that were discussed more than twice:

- Three times: humility, innovation, learning, and passion.
- Four times: communication, fun, and work ethic.
- Five times: authenticity and service.
- Six times: vision.
- Seven times: developing people.
- Ten times: integrity.

The top five values, therefore, were authenticity, service, vision, developing people, and integrity. The two clear messages, however, were that there is no one way to lead and that there are many paths for entering leadership roles.

To provide some context to this diversity of leadership skills and potential paths, we'd like to close with five final examples.

Mike Duke, former CEO of Walmart. Mike grew up in rural Georgia, and he had a family that taught him about love and faith. Mike's leadership journey included contributions from several mentors, from the teachers at Georgia Tech to his supervisor at his first job.

Mike readily admitted that he stumbled as he moved along, and he often felt he wasn't performing very well. He succeeded, however, by learning to focus on whatever role he was in. Rather than thinking about his next job, he channeled his energy into trying to be better at his current tasks—and that typically paid off in new opportunities.

Angela Grayson, principal member and founder of Precipice IP. Angela believes there are many successful leadership principles, but that you can find yourself more enriched when you open your professional and personal world to people who do not look like you.

She suggested performing an easy task to see if you are doing this. Open your LinkedIn account and check your connections. Are they all the same race? All the same gender? From the same political party? You should have a diverse mix. If you do, she believes that you will grow the best and the most.

Troy Alley, executive vice president and chief operating officer of Con-Real. At the end of his discussion with us, Troy took several minutes to emphasize the importance of leading by your values. If you abide by these values, Troy said, you may not be the best financially, but you will be the best person you can be in the world. There are lots of wealthy people, but people often don't remember someone's financial position; however, they will remember who you are, what you've done, how you've improved yourself, and how you've improved the lives of others. He believes that if you can't give to others, you are wasting your time.

Mario Ramirez, president of MRamirez Group. Mario emphasized that students have a great opportunity in front of them. He encouraged them to develop a lot of relationships, as Mario's career is built around relationships. While many relationships are established over your career, they all start with the relationships that you develop as a student. Mario believes that lifelong relationships are not only key to your career, but also beneficial to your life. He ended the discussion by saying "embrace it all and move forward, charge ahead!"

Mike Johnson, former associate vice-chancellor for facilities at the University of Arkansas. Mike pointed out that "current students are our next generation of leaders." He believes that these students will lead us regardless of their similarities and, perhaps more importantly, regardless of their differences—if we can all come together.

This perspective cuts through any potential lens of leadership and gets us to the heart of the matter: the next generation is always coming, and all generations must work together to move everyone in a positive direction.

So what have we learned? Leaders inspire us. We walked away from the podcast interviews saying things like "wow," "humbling," "impressive," and "staggering."

Leaders inspire us because they are nimble. They skillfully navigate uncharted waters.

Leaders inspire us because they never see themselves as finished products. They never stop learning and never tire of doing better.

Leaders inspire us with their integrity. You can put their word in the bank. They execute consistently because of this, and they know their true north.

Leaders inspire us with their sense of vision. They are clear about where they are going and where they want to take their organizations, so their organizations naturally wrap around them.

Leaders inspire us with their humility and presence. When you are talking to a chancellor, a CEO, or a company president, and they consistently say that they are always learning from others, you feel humbled.

Leaders inspire us with their ease in telling stories, applying them to life, and teaching us.

Leaders inspire us with their life-work balance. Again, they are always learning from mistakes.

Leaders inspire us with their empathetic listening skills. They make you feel good about your life and perspectives.

We could go on, because the list is very long, but here's the bottom line: Leaders inspire us with abilities that are learned and not genetically sealed. Therefore, we don't just admire those leaders, we can emulate them. We can develop the traits that make them inspirational, and so can you.

Our challenge is to be authentic in all we do by knowing our values and living by them. In other words, we can't just say that we value integrity, we must lead with integrity—even on seemingly small things like paying $12 for a banana.

We are called to make a positive difference in the lives of others, and we were fortunate to have interviewed twenty-three people who have changed the lives of millions by knowing their values, living them, and leading with authenticity.

The formula isn't complicated. Identify your core values, reflect on how your actions represent those values, and live by the values. This is authentic leadership, and sharing this message was the motivation for recording the LeadershipWWEB podcasts and writing this book—so the next generation (and the ones after that) can learn authentic leadership and pass it along to their successors. That is our challenge. Will you make it yours?

Number of guests (out of 23)	Values
Three	Humility, innovation, learning, and passion
Four	Communication, fun, and work ethic
Five	Authenticity and service
Six	Vision
Seven	Developing people
Ten	Integrity

Table C.1. Values Mentioned by More than Two LeadershipWWEB Podcast Guests

Summary of LeadershipWWEB Podcasts

Date of recording	Interviewee	Position at time of recording	Podcast URL	Interviewer(s)	
10/10/2018	John White	Professor of industrial engineering and chancellor emeritus, University of Arkansas	https://soundcloud.com/user-561194034/chancellor-john-white	John English, Matt Waller	
11/6/2018	Chris McCoy	Vice-chancellor for finance and administration, University of Arkansas	https://soundcloud.com/user-561194034/chris-mccoy	John English, Matt Waller	
11/15/2018	Shelley Simpson	Executive vice president, J. B. Hunt Transport Services	https://soundcloud.com/user-561194034/shelley-simpson	Matt Waller, Andrew Braham	
12/19/2018	Mike Duke	Former president and CEO, Walmart	https://soundcloud.com/user-561194034/mike-duke	John White, John English	
1/8/2019	Donnie Smith	Former CEO, Tyson Foods	https://soundcloud.com/user-561194034/donnie-smith	John White, John English, Andrew Braham	
1/11/2019	Kim LaScola Needy	Professor of industrial engineering and dean of the Graduate School and International Education, University of Arkansas	https://soundcloud.com/user-561194034/kim-needy	John English, Andrew Braham	
1/24/2019	John Reap	Former president and CEO, Town North Bank	https://soundcloud.com/user-561194034/john-reap	John English, Matt Waller, Andrew Braham	

Values				
Empathy	Faith	Flexibility	Integrity	Vision
Collaboration	Community	Creativity	Leadership	Service
Authenticity	Integrity	Leading by example	Passion	Work ethic
Servant	Passion	Innovation	Develop people	Integrity
Authenticity	Courage	Humility	Integrity	Service
Authenticity	Integrity	Make a difference	Respect	Service
Communication	Fair	Fun	Develop people	Vision

Date of recording	Interviewee	Position at time of recording	Podcast URL	Interviewer(s)	
1/24/2019	Troy Alley	Executive vice president and chief operating officer, Con-Real	https:// soundcloud.com /user-561194034 /troy-alley	John English, Andrew Braham	
2/5/2019	John N. Roberts III	President and CEO, J. B. Hunt Transport Services	https:// soundcloud.com /user-561194034 /john-roberts	John White, Andrew Braham	
2/14/2019	Mike Johnson	Associate vice-chancellor for Facilities, University of Arkansas	https:// soundcloud.com /user-561194034 /mike-johnson	John English, Andrew Braham	
2/19/2019	Pam McGinnis	President of global marketing, Phillips 66	https:// soundcloud.com /user-561194034 /pam-mcginnis	John English, Bryan Hill	
3/7/2019	Jessica Hendrix	President and CEO, Saatchi & Saatchi X	https:// soundcloud.com /user-561194034 /jessica-hendrix	Matt Waller, Andrew Braham	
3/15/2019	Angela J. Grayson	Principal member and founder, Precipice IP	https:// soundcloud.com /user-561194034 /angela-grayson	Andrew Braham, Rachel Pohl	
4/2/2019	Anthony J. Vinciquerra	Chairman and CEO, Sony Pictures Entertainment	https:// soundcloud.com /user-561194034 /tony-vinciquerra	John White	
4/12/2019	J. R. Jones	Former CEO and president, Rheem Manufacturing Company	https:// soundcloud.com /user-561194034 /jr-jones	John English, Andrew Braham	
4/24/2019	Greg Brown	Chairman and CEO, Motorola Solutions	https:// soundcloud.com /user-561194034 /greg-brown	John White	

Values				
Commitment	Communication	Confidence	Giving back	Integrity
Clarity of message and direction	Solid, objectives-driven accountability for all	Build, grow, and protect the team	Listen to divergent opinions	Intentional disruption
Commitment	Integrity	Professionalism	Courage	Service
Accountability	Integrity	Reliability	Work ethic	Inclusive
Authenticity	Balance	Learning	Service	Fun
Don't be sorry, take ownership	Ethical	Kind but clear	Try anyway	Work ethic
Highest standards	Always focus on consumer	Top talent	Transparency, openness, and inclusiveness	Collaboration and integration
Accountability	Culture	Develop people	Plan	Vision
Authenticity	Decisive	Judgement	Learning	Work ethic

Date of recording	Interviewee	Position at time of recording	Podcast URL	Interviewer(s)	
5/6/2019	Charles Robinson	Vice-chancellor for the Division of Student Affairs, the University of Arkansas	https:// soundcloud.com /user-561194034 /charles-robinson	Andrew Braham, Sadie Casillas	
5/9/2019	Scott Bennett	Director, Arkansas Department of Transportation	https:// soundcloud.com /user-561194034 /scott-bennett	John English, Andrew Braham	
7/31/2019	Sam Alley	Chairman and CEO, VCC	https:// soundcloud.com /user-561194034 /sam-alley	John English, Andrew Braham	
10/10/2019	Mario Ramirez	President, MRamirez Group	https:// soundcloud.com /user-561194034 /mario-ramirez	Andrew Braham, Sadie Casillas	
10/17/2019	Kelly Barnes	Global and U.S. health industries leader, PwC	https:// soundcloud.com /user-561194034 /kelly-barnes	Matt Waller, Andrew Braham	
12/4/2019	Stu Todd	Founder and managing principal, Compass Partnership Marketing (CPM)	https:// soundcloud.com /user-561194034 /stu-todd-edited	John English, Andrew Braham	

Values				
Communication	Humility	Listen	Empathy	Develop people
Learning	Innovation	Don't be sorry, take ownership	Servant	Develop people
Communication	Decisive	Harmony	Honesty/ integrity	Innovation
Confidence	Humility	Integrity	Loyalty	Preparedness
Choose	Develop people	Fun	Trust	Vision
Compassion	Fun	Merit	Responsibility	Genuine

REFERENCES

Bureau of Labor Statistics. 2020. "Employee Tenure in 2020." https://www.bls
.gov/news.release/pdf/tenure.pdf.

Casari, Marco, Jingjing Zhang, and Christine Jackson. 2012. "When Do Groups
Perform Better Than Individuals? A Company Takeover Experiment."
Working Paper No. 504, Institute for Empirical Research in Economics,
University of Zurich.

Collins, Jim. 2001. *Good to Great: Why Some Companies Make the Leap . . . and
Others Don't*. 1st ed. New York, NY: HarperBusiness.

Drucker, Peter. 1999. "Managing Oneself." *Harvard Business Review* 77: 64–74.

Editors of the Webster's New World Dictionaries, The. 2004. *Webster's New
World College Dictionary*. 4th ed. Cleveland, OH: Wiley Publishing, Inc.

Farber, Steve. 2017 "The Mentoring Checklist: 7 Questions for Finding Someone
to Grow." Inc.com. https://www.inc.com/steve-farber/the-mentoring
-checklist-7-questions-for-finding-someone-to-grow.html.

George, Bill. 2003. *Authentic Leadership: Rediscovering the Secrets to Creating
Lasting Value*. San Francisco, CA: Jossey-Bass.

Goleman, Daniel. 2004. "What Makes a Leader?" *Harvard Business Review* 82
(January): 82–91.

Goulston, Mark. March, 2015. *Just Listen: Discover the Secret to Getting through to
Absolutely Anyone*. New York: AMACOM.

Harvard Business Review. 2011. *HBR's 10 Must Reads on Leadership*. Brighton,
MA: Harvard Business Review Press.

Heifetz, Ronald, and Donald Laurie. 2001. "The Work of Leadership." *Harvard
Business Review* 79 (December): 131–41.

Illinois Leadership Center. 2006a. "Ignite Participant Manual." University of
Illinois at Urbana-Champaign.

Illinois Leadership Center. 2006b. "Intersect Facilitator Manual." University of
Illinois at Urbana-Champaign.

De Janasz, Suzanne, and Maury Peiperl. 2015. "CEOs Need Mentors Too."
Harvard Business Review, April. https://hbr.org/2015/04/ceos-need
-mentors-too.

Koch, Charles. 2007. *The Science of Success: How Market-Based Management
Built the World's Largest Private Company*. Hoboken, NJ: John Wiley and
Sons.

Komives, Susan, Nance Lucas, and Timothy McMahon. 2013. *Exploring Leadership: For College Students Who Want to Make a Difference*. 3rd ed. San Francisco, CA: Jossey-Bass.

Kotter, John P. 1990. *What Leaders Really Do*. 1st ed. Brighton, MA: Harvard Business Review Press.

Kouzes, James, and Barry Posner. 2014. *The Student Leadership Challenge: Five Practices for Becoming an Exemplary Leader*. 2nd ed. San Francisco, CA: Jossey-Bass.

Lawrence, Rich, Molly Rapert, Matt Waller, and Jeff Murray. 2019. "How to Make the Most of Mentoring." *Walton Insights*, November 14. https://walton.uark.edu/insights/good-mentor.php.

MacKenzie, Gordon. 1998. *Orbiting the Giant Hairball: A Corporate Fool's Guide to Surviving with Grace*. New York, NY: Viking.

Marcus, Bernie, and Arthur Blank. 1999. *Built from Scratch: How a Couple of Regular Guys Grew the Home Depot from Nothing to $30 Billion*. New York, NY: Crown Business.

Northouse, Peter. 2018. *Leadership: Theory and Practice*. 8th ed. Thousand Oaks, CA: Sage.

Peters, Tom, and Robert Waterman. 2006. *In Search of Excellence: Lessons from America's Best-Run Companies*. New York, NY: Harper Business.

Phillips, Donald. 1992. *Lincoln on Leadership: Executive Strategies for Tough Times*. New York: Warner Books.

Rakowich, Walt. 2020. *Transfluence: How to Lead with Transformative Influence in Today's Climates of Change*. Franklin, TN: Post-Hill Press.

Sample, Steven. 2003. *The Contrarian's Guide to Leadership*. San Francisco, CA: Jossey-Bass.

Smyth, Lisa. 2017. "Why CEOs Need Mentors Too." *CEO*, June 15. https://www.theceomagazine.com/business/management-leadership/ceos-need-mentors/.

Tyson. n.d. "Purpose and Values." Accessed October 8, 2021. https://www.tysonfoods.com/who-we-are/our-story/purpose-values.

Wagner, Wendy, and Daniel Ostick. 2013. *Exploring Leadership: For College Students Who Want to Make a Difference: Facilitation and Activity Guide*. San Francisco, CA: Jossey-Bass.

Walumbwa, Fred O., Bruce J. Avolio, William L. Gardner, Tara S. Wernsing, and Suzanne J. Peterson. 2008. "Authentic Leadership: Development and Validation of a Theory-Based Measure." *Journal of Management* 34 (1): 89–126.

White, Steve. 2022. *Uncompromising: How an Unwavering Commitment to Your Why Leads to an Impactful Life and a Lasting Legacy*. Franklin, TN: Post Hill Press.

INDEX

Note: Information in tables is indicated by *t* following page number.

Andrew Braham (PhD, University of Illinois) is an associate professor of civil engineering at the University of Arkansas. He was a visiting associate professor at the Polytechnic University of Catalonia, in Barcelona, Spain; a postdoctoral research fellow at Southeast University, in Nanjing, China; and a graduate research assistant at the Illinois Leadership Center. In addition, he worked as a field and research engineer for Koch Materials Company. He coauthored *Fundamentals of Sustainability in Civil Engineering*, created the Pavinar webinar series (which can be found on YouTube), and developed four online certificate programs revolving around asphalt emulsion. He is active in committees of the Transportation Research Board and the Pavement Preservation and Recycling Alliance, as well as various committees and programs at the University of Arkansas.

John English (PhD, Oklahoma State University) is the vice-chancellor for the Division of Research and Innovation at the University of Arkansas, where he also holds the Irma R. and Raymond F. Giffels Endowed Chair in Engineering and is a tenured full professor in the Department of Industrial Engineering. He holds the membership level of fellow in the Institute of Industrial and Systems Engineers, where he has served on the board of trustees and held many other positions, including senior vice president of publications. He is also an elected board member of both the American Society for Engineering Education and the Engineering Dean's Council Executive Board. He is the past general chair and chair of the board of directors of the Reliability and Maintainability Symposium. He served for more than seven years as dean of the College of Engineering at the University of Arkansas. Before that, he was dean of Carl R. Ice College of Engineering at Kansas State University, where he held the LeRoy C. and Aileen H. Paslay Chair in Engineering. He has received awards for teaching and research, including the Dr. Theo Williamson Award for the best paper in integrated manufacturing systems.

Matthew Waller (PhD, Pennsylvania State University) is dean of the Sam M. Walton College of Business at the University of Arkansas, where he also holds the Sam M. Walton Leadership Chair and is a professor of supply chain management. He received the Council of Supply Chain Management Professionals' Distinguished Service Award in 2020 and is the former coeditor in chief of the *Journal of Business Logistics*. In addition to his work in academe, he is a board member of the Winthrop Rockefeller Institute and cofounded Bentonville Associates Ventures and Mercari Technologies. He also is coauthor of *The Definitive Guide to Inventory Management, Purple on the Inside: How J. B. Hunt Transport Set Itself Apart in a Field Full of Brown Cows, Integrating Blockchain into Supply Chain Management: A Toolkit for Practical Implementation,* and *The Dean's List: Leading a Modern Business School.*

Printed in the USA
CPSIA information can be obtained
at www.ICGtesting.com
LVHW031014220324
775005LV00003B/8